THY KINGDOM COME

DESTINY IMAGE BOOKS BY FELIX HALPERN

Dancing Past the Darkness: The Glory Mindset

Living with Heaven's Glory
Mindset: 31 Days of Kingdom Glory

Thy Kingdom Come: The Mystery of Israel's Glory

THY KINGDOM COME

THE MYSTERY OF ISRAEL'S GLORY

FELIX HALPERN

DESTINY IMAGE® PUBLISHERS, INC.

P.O. Box 310, Shippensburg, PA 17257-0310

"Publishing cutting-edge prophetic resources to supernaturally empower the body of Christ"

This book and all other Destiny Image and Destiny Image Fiction books are available at Christian bookstores and distributors worldwide.

For more information on foreign distributors, call 717-532-3040.

Reach us on the Internet: www.destinyimage.com.

ISBN 13 TP: 978-0-7684-7754-2

ISBN 13 eBook: 978-0-7684-7755-9

For Worldwide Distribution, Printed in the U.S.A.

1 2 3 4 5 6 7 8 / 27 26 25 24 23

DEDICATION

THIS BOOK IS LOVINGLY DEDICATED TO MY BELOVED WIFE and partner in ministry, Bonnie, whose unwavering support, strength, and dedication have made this work possible.

I also extend this dedication to my grandson, Hudson Felix, with the hope that he will carry on the honorable legacy of his grandfather and great-grandfather.

I honor the memory of my paternal grandfather, Rabbi Felix Halpern, and the uncles, aunts, and cousins who tragically lost their lives to the Nazis. Furthermore, I pay tribute to my maternal grandparents, who courageously risked everything to lead the Underground Resistance against the Nazis, fighting for the survival of the Jewish people.

CONTENTS

AUTHOR'S NOTE

THROUGH MY RESEARCH ON ANTI-SEMITISM FOR THIS book, I have gained a profound understanding of my own family's history, which has long evoked a subdued response within me. This book is my responsibility to bridge that gap and pay tribute to the Dutch Underground Liberation Movement during the Nazi occupation of Holland.

I cannot overlook the countless sacrifices made by my grandparents, who bravely sheltered Jews in their homes during the dark days of Nazi-occupied Holland. Their dedication called for decisive action, even from their children. Today, some of those who were hidden have led fulfilling lives with their children and grandchildren in Israel.

In the aftermath of the war, it became evident that most people were unwilling to put themselves at risk, let alone endanger the lives of their loved ones, to stand up for the Jewish people. Few were willing to even whisper their dissent. It is a blessing that some individuals possessed the courage to do so.

As a young boy, I was captivated by the many stories that resurfaced, each filled with harrowing details. I recall the times when my grandfather was arrested by the Gestapo, only to experience miraculous deliverance by God. These individuals are truly exceptional, destined to be warriors. True heroes are a rare breed, and we certainly need more of them today! My mother eloquently writes about these heroes in her book, *The War Years:*

> They possessed a strength of character, nerves of steel, and an inner fortitude that most people can only dream of. It was as though they had been trained for battle, though not by any earthly army. In this case, God was their commander-in-chief, empowering them with the strength and courage to carry out perilous missions and achieve success.[1]

While this book primarily focuses on the spiritual liberation of the Jewish people, these personal stories have unexpectedly emerged as a powerful force in my work. Reflecting on the Jewish people and their connection with Gentiles throughout history, I discovered a long-standing and profound providential link between them. Therefore, the coming together of Jews and Gentiles today is a significant marker of our time, presenting new opportunities for transformation and change.

INTRODUCTION

THIS BOOK DOES NOT FOCUS ON ONE SINGLE STORY OR BIB-
lical truth. Rather, it presents pieces of a prophetic puzzle
that unveil God's long-standing plan for the end-time church,
Israel, and the coming Kingdom. It also sheds light on God's
intended relationship between Jews and Gentiles, the church
and the Jewish people, and the long-standing connection
between the church and Israel.

While looking more at early Jewish and Christian think-
ing, the early church gradually distanced itself from any
Jewish awareness and thoughts—the relationship between
Jews and Gentiles—the church and Israel.

Today, we are experiencing a surge of recent and excit-
ing movements of the Spirit that cultivate a sincere affec-
tion for Israel and the Jewish people among the Gentile
Christian church. A more Jewish-centric church continues
to emerge, embracing biblical feasts, shofars sounding, the
revival of Hebrew praise and worship, and the observance of

the Saturday Sabbath. Many are discovering the richness of the Jewish foundation of New Covenant faith.

The words of church historian Emil Schurer accurately describe the experiences of many individuals today:

> Innumerable threads with the previous thousand years Of Israel's history join Christianity and Judaism. No incident in the gospel story, no word in the preaching of the Messiah, is intelligible apart from its history and without a clear understanding of that world of thought distinction of the Jewish people.[1]

With much of our attention given to the Institutional church, we explore key historical events in Jewish history that reframed Judaism for generations. One was the Roman invasion of Jerusalem in AD 70. One million Jews were sent to their deaths, 97,000 Jews were captured, and thousands were sold as slaves throughout the cities of the Roman Empire. Thousands more perished from starvation... Judaism was on the brink of extinction again.[2]

Legend has it that Jerusalem's spiritual leader at the time, Rabbi Yochanan ben Zakkai, knew certain resistance was futile. He then had his followers secretly carry him out of the city in a coffin, so he could appeal to the Roman commander to let him and some of his sages go to Yavneh, a city east of Jerusalem.

Given permission, Rabbi ben Zakkai established a new learning institution where matters of law were reorganized. Legal and spiritual rulings were disseminated throughout the Diaspora as Jews began to turn to Yavneh for guidance and leadership. His new system was built upon good deeds and studying the Torah. His followers were taught that these elements were more pleasing to God. This early movement and restructuring of Judaism formed the basis for today's rabbinic Judaism.

INSTITUTIONAL CHRISTIANITY

To the subject of the early Christian church, or Institutional Christianity, we explore key episodes of anti-Semitism, thereby creating a historical divide between the Jew and Gentile, the church and Israel, throughout the church age.

Influential individuals emerged that prejudiced the early church toward Jews. Their ingrained prejudice and distorted theological beliefs (replacement theology, supersessionism, dispensationalism) led successive generations astray from understanding the true nature of the divine bond between Jews and Gentiles. This flawed perception served as a foundation for Jewish-Christian relations over two millennia. One absurd idea was that God had irreversibly forsaken His chosen people, rendering any hope of reconciliation futile.

Thank God, many have awakened to the truth and now grasp the concept that the New Covenant faith is as Jewish as the Old; one body of truth intended to include Jews from the early days of Messiah's coming and up to the present.

With the emergence of these new perspectives, we must remain vigilant as the alarming resurgence of anti-semitism and the spreading of the influence of replacement theology today.

The "One New Man" is another profound concept with immense relevance, much like in the time of the apostle Paul. Countless individuals are now gaining a deeper comprehension of the Kingdom by observing the unity between Jews and Gentiles as God intended. As Paul fervently embraced the one new man in his era, a contemporary move of a new understanding of this truth is underfoot in our current time. This mysterious design is explicitly referenced in the Scriptures.

We plumb the depths of this *mystery,* only to find ourselves in Genesis 17, where God's miraculous dealings with Abraham are found. In actuality, the first prototypical model of the one new man is discovered, as well as some of the best touchstones to understand the establishment of the Jewish people.

Final Mandate

The subjects explored in this work—Jewish survival, the church's ultimate mission, and the unity of Jews and Gentiles in the last days—have been at the center of contention and debate for centuries. The Jewish people have endured persecution and faced the threat of annihilation by various nations. This leads us to question the origin of this deep-rooted anti-Semitism that has persisted through the ages.

Why have Jews been subjected to expulsions from countless nations? Why have they been targeted with ridicule for their religious fervor and marked as convenient scapegoats for economic difficulties throughout history? *Thy Kingdom*

Come delves into these inquiries, shedding light on a remarkable foreshadowing of the forthcoming Kingdom.

Readers will gain a renewed perspective on the future of the church, the millennial reign of the Messiah, and the intertwined roles of Jews and Gentiles in God's grand plan for the end times. Above all, this work underscores the inseparable and enduring connection between Jews and Gentiles throughout eternity.

PART I

THE JEWS AND ISRAEL

1

JERUSALEM AND THE LAND OF ISRAEL

Jerusalem does not cease being to the Jewish people, it was during King David's time and still is today; Jerusalem is the heart of the Jewish people and its joy. It has been designated [by the United Nations Special Commission on Palestine, 1947] the capital of the Jewish state. Still, it was and will always remain the capital of the Jewish people, the core of the entire Jewish people.[1]

—DAVID BEN GURION,
First Prime Minister of Israel

OUR STUDY BEGINS WITH THE LAND GOD BESTOWED UPON the Jewish people, as it remains the foundation of their heritage going back to ancient times.

Throughout the Bible, this land is referred to by various names: the land of the Hebrews (Genesis 40:15), the

Holy Land (Zechariah 2:12), the land of Jehovah (Hosea 9:3, Psalm 85:1), and the land of Promise (Hebrews 11:9). However, the term Promised Land succinctly captures its essence, tracing its significance back to God's covenant with Abraham, his descendants, and subsequent generations.

It is important to note. The Jewish people settled the land some 3,200 years ago, approximately 1200 BCE (Before Common Era or Before Christ), when Joshua conquered the Promised Land. Therefore, it was long before the Arab conquest of Jerusalem in the year 640, or the conquest of the Ottoman Turks in 1516.

When King David first purchased the threshing floor from Ornan (2 Chronicles 3) for what would become the Temple Mount, he could never have known the political and spiritual contention it would become.

In that place, also called Mount Moriah, King Solomon built the house of the Lord; Abraham came close to sacrificing Isaac; and the Lord appeared unto David, the father of Solomon. But it has remained at the center of a historical and spiritual struggle ever since. The eternal battle for it will end only when it has reached its final state under the reign of the Messiah.

When a great scholar and sage of the thirteenth century, Rabbi Moshe ben Nachman, states, "To take possession of the Holy Land and to live in it must be counted amongst the Biblical commandments incumbent upon Jews to fulfill," an unmistakable connection was made between the Jewish people and Jerusalem for generations. Therefore, the birth of Israel in 1948 was the most significant prophetic event in modern history; and for the non-Jewish world, Israel remains the axis for end-time events.

ABRAHAM, THE CHOSEN STEWARD

It all started with Abraham. He was the chosen intermediary between God and the covenant and for his seed. He was also a descendant of Eber, an Eberite. Eber means to "cross over" because Abram (Abraham) crossed over from the other side east of the Euphrates River. Eber was also the great-grandson of Shem and the ancestor of Yeshua (Genesis 10:21; Luke 3:35).

Ancestrally speaking then, Eber was the founder of the Hebrew race we call Jews today (Luke 3:35). However, Jews trace their lineage not back to Eber but to Abraham—the nations also receive their connection to Abraham (Galatians 3:29).

Abraham's grandson Jacob came to be known as Israel, and his twelve sons formed the twelve tribes of Israel. They were Reuben, Simeon, Levi, Judah, Issachar, Zebulon, Dan, Naphtali, Gad, Asher, Joseph, and Benjamin (Genesis 29:32-34; 35:16-18). The tribe of Judah, however, became the most prominent of the twelve tribes, of which the Messianic line would be established, and the leading tribe of Israel.

ISRAEL'S FIRST VISIONARY

Divine Providence has consistently called upon extraordinary individuals to fulfill significant roles throughout history. Among them, Abraham stands out as the chosen one who initiated the course of Jewish history. Moses was specifically selected to guide the Israelites to Mount Sinai, and Joshua emerged as their leader, guiding them into the long-awaited Promised Land.

In a parallel vein, Theodor Herzl (1860-1904) played a pivotal role in leading the Jewish people back to the land promised to them after two millennia of wandering. Herzl's visionary efforts paved the way for a new chapter in Jewish history, setting the stage for the realization of prophetic fulfillment in a fresh era.

THEODOR HERZL

Theodor Herzl, hailing from a prosperous banking family, made a significant life choice by pursuing a career in journalism and relocating to Vienna to work for a local newspaper. During his coverage of the trial of a Jewish French captain falsely accused of divulging French military secrets to Germany, Herzl found himself exposed to unsettling anti-Jewish sentiments and fervent public demonstrations.

The shocking chants of *"A bas les Juifs"* (meaning, "Down with the Jews") and *"A la mort les Juifs"* ("Death to the Jews"), left an indelible impact on Herzl, leading him to the realization that the eradication of hatred toward Jews was an improbable feat. He believed, at best, that it could only be mitigated. Thus, his proposed solution came in the form of a Zionist state.

In 1896, Herzl published a book outlining this idea titled *Der Judenstat* (The Jewish State) Project. The next year under his leadership, the First Zionist Congress convened in Basel, Switzerland. At that time, many were what Herzl considered *oppositionists* and *assimilationists*—people more concerned with the loss of Jewish wealth than the safety of the Jewish people. Then Nazi Germany rose to power, and Herzl's worst fears were realized.

Despite opposition, his determination led to a coalition of nations that finally agreed that the Jews needed a safe haven to call their own, which took place on November 29, 1947. But linked to the United Nations (UN) agreement was a vision for two independent states to bring about the internationalization of Jerusalem.

Throughout the process, Arab intentions were known that war would follow if Israel were granted her land. Still, on May 14, 1948, Israel finally declared its independence. As expected, the allied forces of Syria, Lebanon, Jordan, Egypt, and Iraq attacked Israel the following day in defiance of the UN agreement. Unprepared due to an international arms embargo, Czechoslovakia eventually aided Israel by selling her arms and supplies, which turned the tide of the war in Israel's favor—of course, God would have raised up another nation.

JERUSALEM: THE CITY OF PEACE DEFINED BY WAR

Jerusalem, known as the city of God, holds a unique status as a highly revered and contested land for nations worldwide. According to the belief held by rabbis, Jews experienced profound spiritual achievements on two occasions—the construction of the Temples—only to witness their destruction, both tragically coinciding with the ninth of AV (Tisha B'Av).

Since 1948 and the War of Independence, Israel has experienced many wars. In her early history came the war of the Sinai Campaign in 1956 between Israel and Egypt; then the Six Day War in 1967 with Nasser of Egypt, Jordan, and Syria; the Yom Kippur War in 1973, when Egyptian and Syrian forces attacked Israel on two fronts.

While Israel has endured two intifadas and lives under continuous threats of terrorism, she continually experiences diplomatic isolation when she seeks to protect herself. Israel is roughly 8,500 square miles today, a mere fraction of its original 60,000 square miles when David and his son Solomon reigned. Israel still struggles to retain its fullness of it.[2]

Why is a small state, both in land and population, despised by so many? The answer is not found in the geopolitical sphere but within the spiritual sphere. Israel is the future resting place of the Throne of God, where the coming Kingdom of Heaven will administer its government.

Therefore, the Jewish people are emotionally, spiritually, prophetically, and biblically connected to their land. In the words of Rabbi Hayim Halevy Donin, "It is a land possessed by not only right of conquest and settlement but also a fulfillment of history, faith, and law."[3]

2

JEWISH PERSECUTION: THE STRATEGY OF SATAN

Israel is likened to a man traveling on the road when he encountered a wolf and escaped from it, and he went along relating the affair of the wolf. He then encountered a lion, escaped from it, and related the affair of the lion. He then encountered a snake and escaped from it, forgot the two previous incidents, and went along relating the affair of the snake. So it is with Israel; the present troubles cause them to forget the earlier one.[1]

—BERKOTH 13A

THROUGHOUT HISTORY, IT HAS BECOME EVIDENT THAT satan has persistently sought to annihilate the Jewish people. This dynamic is exemplified in the scriptural depiction of the relationship between Israel and its adversary, Aram (Syria), likened to water and fire. A prophecy concerning Damascus in Isaiah 17:12 warns of the tumultuous roar of many nations, while Obadiah compares the Jewish people to fire in Obadiah 1:18.

This simple analogy sheds light on a well-established biblical truth: the Jewish people were intended to be a source of fire and light, spreading the illumination of the One True God and His Kingdom principles to the world. However, numerous nations have tried suppressing the Jewish people, like water extinguishing fire. This statement may appear harsh, but it is grounded in centuries of anti-Semitic acts that have left little to the depths of the human imagination: the Holocaust, blood libels, forced conversions, exiles, and expulsions.

In light of this historical backdrop, one must ask whether it is possible to truly develop a compassionate heart for the Jewish people without comprehending their long-standing suffering and persecution, particularly when such persecution has often been perpetrated under the banner of Christianity, a religion tainted by anti-Semitism. The answer, unequivocally, is no.

Therefore, provided is a brief overview to familiarize readers with the seven distinct categories of anti-Semitic acts committed against Jews.

EXILES MARCHING THROUGH TIME

Because Jews have been exiled and unwelcomed in most places—scattered and wandering for thousands of years—Jews can be found in virtually every nation on earth. History reveals that few nations are free from the particular Jewish bloodguilt of being unwelcoming to Jewish people.

Taking the most basic treatment of this subject, European nations such as England, France, Germany, Portugal, Spain, Lithuania, and Hungary displaced thousands of Jews. In 1492, more than 90,000 Jews from Turkey were forced to leave their homes. In that same period, thousands were forcibly baptized in Spain, and those who refused were exiled.

Combined, hundreds of thousands of Jews were displaced, thousands died seeking a new home, and untold thousands more were converted and baptized into Christianity.[2] One can only imagine what Spanish Jewry thought at the time of the Jewish Psalm 60:1 (KJV): *"O God, thou hast cast us off, thou hast scattered us, thou hast been displeased; O turn thyself to us again."*

THE HORROR OF THE POGROMS

Pogrom is a Russian word that means riot or devastation and applies to violent anti-Jewish attacks. Hundreds of pogroms on a large scale brought massacres of Jewish people and anti-Jewish riots that took place, especially under the Czarist regime of Russia and Poland.

The most severe pogroms occurred in 1881 and 1903, then from 1918 to 1921. These riots were highly organized to devastate Jewish neighborhoods, including the burning of synagogues and the beating of Jews to the point of death.

ALWAYS BRANDED AS DIFFERENT

Jews have long been branded by society as different. Whether they are portrayed as modern-day money mongers or from old fables describing them as people who have horns. When Jews were forced to wear special labels to tell them apart from Gentiles, it began a notorious and demeaning practice.

In 1215, a decree was issued at the 4th Lateran Council that all Jews were required to wear a yellow badge upon their breast to distinguish them from Gentile Christians. In 1317, the Catholic Church at the Ravenna Council declared the following:

> They (Jews) ought not to be tolerated to the detriment or severe injury of the faithful because they frequently return to Christians contumely for favors, familiarity contempt.
>
> To prevent them from deceiving the flocks by their poisoned words and immoral conduct, they dress and shall, when in public places and during their journeys, distinguish themselves from other people by a peculiar shape and dress color; i.e. a wheel-like badge.
>
> At the provincial of Ravenna some time since... thinking that many scandals have arisen from them commingling with Christians, it is decreed that they should wear a wheel of yellow cloth on their outer garment, and their women alike

wheel on their heads, so that they may be distinguished from Christians.[3]

This decree was extended beyond Italian territories during the papacy of Pope Innocent III. There is also record of Jews being required to wear a badge elsewhere in Europe, including England by Edward II.

The badge or patch became an internationally recognized identifier of Jewish communities. The shape and color of the badge or patch could vary; in some instances, the color yellow became the standard throughout Europe in place of the wheel patch. The yellow badges were levied as punishment by both the Catholic Church and civil governments and could include fines and other punitive measures.

The badges served as a visual reminder to Jews and Christians of their separation, but also to remind Jews of their status as second-class citizens in many places across Europe. The badges remained a symbol of oppression for centuries and a reminder of how Jews were treated different from their Christian neighbors in medieval Europe. The oppressive system of Jews wearing badges as a form of public humiliation and guilt was eventually abolished following the French Revolution.

OTHER SIGNIFICANT RULINGS, HAPPENINGS, AND DATES

Years: Events

589: The Council of Toledo forbade Jews from holding public office.

612–621: King Sisebut demanded either baptism or exile.

570–636: Saint Isidore of Sevilla forbade forced baptisms, but if Jewish children were baptized to save their lives, they had to be taken from their parents and reared Catholic. (In some situations, Jewish people were given a choice of baptism or death.)

1095–1096: First Crusade against the Jews, killing those who refused baptism.

1147–1149: Second Crusade, the same took place.

1357 to 1351: During the Black Death plague, Jews were accused of poisoning the wells, thus causing the plague. Some of this may have come from the fact that many Jewish people were observing the health laws of Tanakh and were thus not getting sick (Toledo, 681).[4]

Christians were not permitted to patronize Jewish doctors (Trulanic Synod, 692).

Jews were required to pay taxes for the support of the Roman Church.

Christians were prohibited from attending Jewish ceremonies (Synod of Vienna, 1267).

Compulsory ghettos (Synod of Breslau, 1267).

Jews were not allowed to obtain academic degrees (Council of Basel, X Session IX).[5]

One can easily see some of Hitler's inspiration when he reinstituted the Nazi policy of labeling the Jews during the Holocaust. Hitler brought the practice to new heights, however, when he posted reminders throughout Germany: "When you see this symbol [the yellow star,] know your true enemy."

FORCED CONVERSIONS ON JEWISH CHILDREN

In the context of such persecutions in the name of Christianity, Judaism began to see it as a religion that brought great suffering to the Jewish people. Imagine taking Jewish children, with complete disregard for their parents, to convert them. The forced conversion occurred throughout Europe, Persia, and Morocco, particularly from the years 460 to 1858. It occurred again in Morocco in 1145 when Jews were forced to convert to Islam.

The most notorious was the Canonist decree during the nineteenth century by Russian authorities. Children were seized and forced to serve in the czar's army and then shipped off to distant locations for as many as twenty-five years. Jewish children were forced to lose all contact with their people to assimilate and convert to the local religion.

In 1242, the Jews of Spain were forced to attend conversion sermons by order of King James I of Aragon, while massive burnings of the Talmud took place in Paris during this time.

Finally, an event in England in 1222 characterizes the social paranoia and hatred against the Jew, when a young university student was burned alive for marrying a Jew and converting to Judaism.

The central prayer of *Kol Nidre* that is recited during Yom Kippur renounces all pledges that captors and misled Christian zealots forced upon the Jew:

> Kol Nidre: All vows, oaths, and pledges which we may be forced to take between this Yom Kippur and the next, of these, we repent, and these, we renounce. Let them be nullified and voided and let us be absolved and released. Let personal vows, pledges, be considered neither vows, nor pledges, nor oaths.

THEY FALSELY ACCUSED US

Historically, a blood libel is a lie or fable that accuses Jews of taking a Christian child's blood for ritual purposes, specifically, to make matzo for Passover.

As ridiculous as these charges sound, many believed it. *Blood libel* fantasies became a regular charge from Christian anti-Semites during the Middle Ages. So rampant was it that the Muslim world repeated it by substituting a Muslim child for a Christian child and *hamantaschen* for *matzo*.

The first recorded *blood libel* took place in England in the year 1144. It was a twelve-year-old English boy whose violent death was attributed to the Jewish community of Norwich merely because he regularly came into contact with Jews; his name was William of Norwich. Later, he was venerated as a martyr, though his death was never solved.

Nevertheless, the allegation of ritual murder or *blood libel* was believed to cause his death. Hitler renewed the superstition of the *blood libel* when on May 1, 1934, in the Nazi Newspaper *der Sturmer,*[6] he devoted the regular weekly edition to this Jewish ritual by posting illustrations of rabbis sucking the blood of German children.

Shocking as this may be, the leader of Hamas, Osama Hamden, stated on August 14, 2014, while interviewed by CNN, "We all remember how the Jews used to slaughter Christians to mix their blood in their holy matzo."

Tribunals

Of all the violent actions against the Jews, perhaps the most feared and hated word is *inquisition*, it means "inquiry." For Gentiles, it also symbolized extremism, ruthlessness, and torture.

In the thirteenth century, church courts were formed to investigate Christian believers; often, they were hunted down and accused of being heretics. For Jews, though, so-called church officials would enter synagogues on Saturday with an armed mob behind them. Jews were then interrogated and pressured to convert, and rarely could Jews argue or refuse this forced conversion method during this time.

Crusades

The Crusades, or "holy wars," ended ten centuries of comparative peace for the Jewish people and ushered in a period of rarely seen persecution.

Launched to cleanse the Holy Land of Jews and Muslims, these so-called "missions from God" incited entire mobs to massacre Jewish communities. "Before attempting to revenge ourselves upon the Muslim unbelievers, let us first revenge ourselves upon the 'killers of Christ' living in our midst," was their battle cry.

It was said, "So great was the killing and the torturing, so great was the Jew's bravery in accepting pain and death without denying their God, that an entire generation died *al Kiddush Ha-Shem,* for the sanctification of God's name."

The first Crusades occurred in 1096, with more Crusades in 1146, 1187, and 1202. The Crusades became internationalized in 1078 when Pope Gregory VII forbade any Christian kingdom from hiring Jews. The principal demand always placed upon the Jews was to accept baptism; though in most cases, Christian conversion only allowed one to die a quicker death.

Annihilation Campaigns

Many attempts have taken place to annihilate the Jewish people, not going back thousands of years, only over the past 350 years to date.

Though no persecution in Jewish history is greater and more infamous than the Holocaust, one of two central campaigns also launched against the Jew was the Chmelnitsky massacre that few, including Jews, are aware of. This atrocity took place in Eastern Europe from 1648 to 1649 and reveals a barbaric treatment of the Jewish people that defies the imagination.

Some of them (the Jews) had their skins flayed off them and their flesh flung to the dogs. The hands and feet of the others were cut off, flung onto the roadway where carts ran over them, and they were trodden underfoot by horse. And many were buried alive, children were slaughtered in their mother's bosom, and many children were torn apart like fish. They ripped up the bellies of pregnant women, took out the unborn children, and flung them in their faces. They tore open the bellies of some of them, placed a living cat within the belly, and left them alive.

The Holocaust

Although one has called the Holocaust the emptying of a great moral space from the world, Hitler had a solution to solve what he saw as the Jewish problem, the "final solution." He planned to exterminate all of European Jewry, and he almost succeeded. Six million Jewish lives were lost. Some of those who died were my paternal grandparents, uncles, aunts, and cousins, and untold other Jewish families the same.

Hitler's propaganda machine claimed that the vileness of Jews was part of their blood; that they were inferior physically, mentally, and culturally. Jews, he said, "polluted modern life with filth and decease. They poisoned others with germs but somehow managed to preserve themselves." Hitler infected German society with Jewish hate to such a degree that a board game was created for Germans called Jews Get Out. This game was sold throughout Germany in 1939 and 1940.

In 1938, a children's anti-Semitic book titled *The Poisonous Mushroom* was published, through which German children could be inculcated with Jewish hate. Throughout Germany, public signs warned women and girls to watch out for the rapist, the Jew! Other public signs were posted stating: "Beware of Jews and pickpockets."

Hitler enacted four hundred laws and decrees defining a "non-Aryan": A non-Aryan was anyone descended from non-Aryan, predominantly Jewish, parents or grandparents, even if only one parent or grandparent was a non-Aryan. Following this policy, every government worker in Germany had to prove his or her lineage.[7]

The Holocaust was a vile genocide, the attempt to annihilate an entire people due to their faith, ethnicity, and supposed inferiority. It was not only a crime against the Jews, but a crime against humanity itself.

In the wake of the Holocaust, new laws were implemented to protect people internationally. The United Nations passed the Convention on the Prevention and Punishment of the Crime of Genocide. The international criminal court and the Universal Declaration of Human Rights were established. These laws and declarations implemented by the United Nations serve to protect all individuals from the injustices suffered by the Jewish people during the Holocaust.

The heinous acts committed during the Holocaust and its ramifications clearly show the need for greater vigilance and respect for the Jewish people. We must always remember the lessons of the Holocaust to teach us that hatred, discrimination, and prejudice should be rejected and never tolerated.

3

JEWISH IMMIGRATION: JEWS COME TO AMERICA

JEWISH IMMIGRATION HAS BEEN CHARACTERIZED BY shared experiences of being unwelcome wherever they have sought to settle. But as America emerged as a refuge for various ethnic groups, during pre-colonial times, the Jewish people also sought a haven for religious freedom. History reveals, however, that America needed to be fully prepared to embrace the Jewish population.

Although America came to be known as a "melting pot," an interesting fact is that Israel Zangwill, a Jewish playwright from England, originally coined the term. Zangwill shared a similar perspective to Theodore Herzl when he portrayed his vision of a Zionist state.

In 1896, Herzl published a work titled *The Jewish State*, in which he presented two options: 1) Jews should either choose national existence in Palestine or 2) assimilate and integrate into society, normalizing their identity to become like everyone else.

Zangwill's 1914 drama, "The Melting Pot," depicted an interfaith couple, one Jewish and one Christian, as a means of bridging the notable differences among Americans. He envisioned the New World, America, as surpassing the glory of Rome or Jerusalem because it became a place where "all races and nations come to labor and look forward to."

Jews Begin to Arrive

The roots of Jewish immigration in America can be traced back to April 1654, when a fleet of sixteen ships was preparing to depart from the harbor of Recife, Brazil. Among the passengers were approximately one hundred and fifty Jewish families, primarily descendants of the Marranos who had escaped the Spanish and Portuguese Inquisition and sought refuge in Brazil.

Due to circumstances that forced them to leave Brazil or convert to Catholicism, these families made the difficult decision to leave their homes and belongings behind in search of religious freedom. Initially, their intended destination was Holland, often referred to as Old Amsterdam, which happens to be my birthplace.

Among the fleet, the ship named St. Charles encountered a devastating incident. Pirates attacked the vessel during the voyage, robbing the passengers of their money and possessions. In need of funds to continue their journey, the ship's captain redirected their course to New Amsterdam, which would later become Manhattan Island. The captain planned to demand payment upon their arrival or even imprison these early Jewish immigrants.

However, a miraculous turn of events occurred. The captain of a French vessel captured the pirates and recovered the stolen money and belongings of the Jewish passengers. Without this act of kindness, they would have certainly faced imprisonment.

During this early period, American settlers were primarily farmers and ranchers known for their ruggedness and hard work. In contrast, the early Jewish immigrants were more inclined toward urban life, often engaged in business and artisanal trades. Although they worked just as hard, their endeavors were directed differently. However, many early American settlers perceived the Jews as benefiting from the labor of others.

Furthermore, America was regarded as a new Christian nation, and the Jews were still associated with the label of "Christ-killers," originating from former England. In fact, Jews were initially prohibited from voting in early colonial America until New York became the first state to grant them voting rights.

These attitudes and prejudices characterized the early American frontier for Jewish settlers. They were consistently viewed as a distinct and different group in need of assimilation, often remedied through conversion to Christianity.

PEOPLE AND PLACES OF INTEREST

Many historical examples can be given that illustrate the difficulties early Jewish settlers experienced. Here we highlight prominent individuals in United States history who lent to early anti-Semitism, which became a pretext for the Jewish experience in early America.

One example is Peter Stuyvesant, the first governor of New Amsterdam, which became known as Manhattan. On September 22, 1654, he petitioned the Dutch West India Company, his employer, to rid his new island of the Jews. But because the company had large Jewish investors, they opposed his appeal.

Still, from then on, Stuyvesant continually sought ways to make the Jews feel unwelcome. He called them repugnant, deceitful enemies, and blasphemers of Christ. He even went as far as to refer to them as "Christ Killers." In his appeal, he wrote the following:

> We have, for the benefit of this week and newly developing place and the land in general, deemed it useful to require them (the Jews) in a friendly way to depart; also praying most seriously in this connection, for ourselves as also for the general community of your worships, that the deceitful race—such hateful enemies and blasphemers of the name of Christ—be not allowed to infect further and trouble this new colony.[1]

Puritans

In Boston, where the Puritans settled, they thought that they were the real Jews and genuine heirs of the promises that God gave to the Jews. Three generations after the beginning of the northern colonies, Samuel Willard outlined Puritan sentiments in a sermon that he preached in 1700:

"The Jews were a scorn and reproach to the world: the happy day of the conversion could improve their condition."[2] The Puritans saw the "end of days" upon them and believed the second coming could not happen unless most Jews were converted.

Hannah Adams

A descendant of Henry Adams and a distant cousin of US President John Adams, Hannah Adams published a work on the history of the Jews in 1812. In her view of history, the suffering of the Jews is due to their rejection of Christ. Adams accuses the Jews of considering themselves "the chosen people" and "superior to all others."[3] More important, what Hannah Adams believed was the general view in America— that American freedom for the Jews was an opportunity for them to be converted to an enlightened Christianity.

Thomas Jefferson

One of America's founders revealed ambivalence toward the Jews when he said, "They should labor to achieve equality in science that is in secular learning so that they will become objects of respect and favor."[4] Later, he was more positive toward them and their religious rights, especially after the

Bill of Rights and the Constitution. Thomas Jefferson was, in fact, the one who incorporated the principle of separation of church and state into the Constitution. He said, "Building a wall of separation between church and state, and that religion is a matter solely between man and God."[5]

Henry Ford

The great American automaker and industrialist was a major trumpet of anti-Semitism in his day. The Protocols of the Elders of Zion, published a generation earlier and most likely by the secret police of the Russian czar, was aimed at justifying anti-Semitic policies and was published in the United States in 1919. Henry Ford financed the production of hundreds of thousands of copies. The publication asserted that the Jews were part of a conspiracy to dominate the world. On this basis, Ford's paper became the chief voice of anti-Semitism in America in the 1920s.

Yale and Harvard

Education for Jewish people was always a high priority, and entering prominent institutions of higher learning before the early 1920s went largely unhindered. A problem began when many universities started to feel uneasy with an increasing Jewish presence as Jews began to outperform their Gentile classmates.

Quotas soon began to be instituted in places like Harvard, Princeton, and Yale. Harvard President A. Lawrence Lowell said in 1922, "If every college in the country would take a limited proportion of Jews, we should go a long way toward eliminating race feeling amongst our students." Lowell was later forced to retract his statement, but Jewish enrollment was mysteriously curtailed sharply after the incident.

At Yale, a decision was made to admit students based on character rather than just scholarship. Dean Frederick Jones at Yale University found that a Jew won almost every single scholarship of any value. He stated, "In terms of scholarship and intelligence, Jewish students lead the class, but their characteristics make them markedly inferior." Of course, this so-called inferiority could only be remedied by conversion to Christianity.[6]

Regarding medical schools, Jewish enrollment was discouraged, and Jewish quotas forced thousands to go abroad for medical training. During the turn of the century, Gentiles controlled virtually all hospitals and the medical profession. It was almost impossible for a Jewish doctor to join a hospital staff or find a Jewish professor in an American medical school. Consequently, the field was virtually closed to Jewish students seeking medical degrees.

LEO FRANK: THE ONLY JEW HUNG IN AMERICA

Perhaps the darkest period of anti-Semitism in America was the Leo Frank case, the only Jew hung in America. Frank was a simple factory worker accused of killing a young woman named Mary Phagan on August 17, 1915, in Marietta, Georgia.

Convicted and condemned to life in prison, the crowds were unsatisfied with his sentence, so they organized themselves into a group called the Knights of Mary Phagan.

Driving to the prison where Frank was held, they forcefully removed him from his prison cell and returned to Marietta, where he was hung from a tree until dead; Leo Frank was the only known Jew ever lynched on American soil.

The case was so sensationalized that stores sold out of rope because people began carrying lengths of rope as memorabilia. Branches of the tree where Frank was hanged were cut down and kept as souvenirs. This incident in Jewish American history gave birth to the Anti-Defamation League of the *B'nai B'rith*.

In 1982, nearly seventy years later, a man known as Alonzo Mann volunteered that he saw Jim Conley carrying Mary Phagan's body at the factory where Frank worked. On March 11, 1986, Leo Frank received a posthumous pardon from the Georgia State Board of Pardons and Paroles and was declared innocent. On March 7, 2008, a historical marker was placed in front of the building at 1200 Roswell near where Frank was killed.[7]

ANTI-SEMITISM IS A SPIRITUAL SICKNESS

Again and again, history has shown that anti-Semitism is not a sickness of just one nation or religion but a condition that crosses all religions and nations. Multitudes of nations have sanctioned and condoned it within their borders. Harvard psychologist Gordon Allport explained anti-Semitism in 1953 when he attributed it to an illness. He stated in his book, The Nature of Prejudice, "Prejudiced people are psychologically abnormal."[8] As a consequence of his published thought on anti-Semitism, Jew-haters were pronounced sick. But this was simply a graceful rationalization for Jewish hatred. Anti-Semitism is a spiritual sickness. It is a grave error to attribute it to a psychological illness since it is rooted in a satanic conspiracy to destroy the elected of God.

4

PRINCIPLES OF ZION: BIBLICAL PRINCIPLES OF JEWISH SURVIVAL

IN THIS CHAPTER, WE EXPLORE THE ESTABLISHMENT OF the foundation by God through Abraham and his descendants. This foundation was meant to be respected by the entire world. The Covenant between God and Abraham is a fundamental cornerstone that extends to the nation of Israel, the world, and the church, known as the New Covenant body. Its origins can be traced back approximately 3,500 years—not just 2,000 years ago.

The Abrahamic covenant serves as a testament to the special relationship between God, His chosen people, and the land of Israel. However, it has also presented challenges and difficulties for other nations throughout history.

Nevertheless, we are currently witnessing a resurgence of interest in the principles of the covenant. Within the global Christian church, there is a gradual decline in anti-Jewish theologies and mindsets as people become more aware of the Jewish roots of the New Covenant faith, Christianity. This holds great significance at this particular time and aligns with the ultimate mission of the non-Jewish Christian community.

PRINCIPLES OF ZION

The Principles of Zion take us beyond the covenant to a kind of insurance policy that ensures God's enduring covenant with the Jewish people.

The first principle revolves around the actual promise that God bestowed upon Abraham. This promise is reinforced by what I refer to as the "terms of power," which outline specific characteristics of the covenant.

The second principle is enforcing the covenant by God, who provides abundant promises and assurances for Jewish survival. As it is written, *"God is not a man, that He should lie, nor a son of man, that He should repent. Has He said, and will He not do? Or has He spoken, and will He not make it good?"* (Numbers 23:19 NKJV).

The third principle stands on the evidence of Jewish history, showcasing the Jewish people's remarkable resilience in the face of adversity. This is known as the law of self-evidence.

The fourth principle centers on the angel of the Lord, a majestic figure in Scripture who serves as a divine messenger and guardian of God's Word. He frequently watches over Israel and the Jewish people.

The fifth and final principle demonstrates that everything God does, He does for His name's sake. For this very reason, Israel endures, and it will forever be a testament to the honor of His great name.

COVENANT AND TERMS OF POWER

No topic is more central to the survival of the Jewish people than the first principle mentioned, the covenant. The Bible has long conveyed a message of warning for nations when their treatment toward the Jew violates God's Word (Genesis 12:3). We will elaborate upon this in a subsequent principle.

The Abrahamic covenant unified God with the Jewish people for all time. It formed a unique bond and history between a people and our Creator.

When God appeared to Abram, He revealed the Promised Land that He had chosen for Abram and his descendants. God made a promise, saying that He would give Abram and his offspring all the land that he saw forever (Genesis 13:15-17).

Additionally, God instructed Abram to explore the length and breadth of the land because He was granting it to him (Genesis 13:15-17). These words from the foundation of the covenant are described in Genesis 15:18-21. This set the stage for a remarkable journey of a people who spanned not just hundreds, but thousands of years, encompassing all the generations that followed as descendants of Abraham. The covenant's official ceremony can be found in Genesis 17:1-8.

More clarification is provided in Leviticus 25:23-24. The God of Abraham and his descendants states that the land was

His, and He would allow them to enter it as "stewards." This is an important light on the covenant land we discover as we proceed.

When the second-generation nation of Israel is ready to cross the Jordan after the first generation wandered for forty years and died, Moses, Joshua, and Caleb are at the Jordan, ready again to seize the Promised Land (Deuteronomy 29:2-3, 10-15).

It may seem like a simple account of biblical history, but it reveals a profound truth. Covenant blessings and provisions operate as a permanent trust; when any Jewish generation chooses to be faithful and obey its conditions, they will receive the blessings, promises, and benefits. So it was with this second generation standing at the Jordan and all future generations.

THE COVENANT'S LEGAL AUTHORITY

In reviewing the Abrahamic Covenant, a legal perspective is taken due to its legal nature. I liken the Covenant to such instruments as the Constitution of the United States, the Bill of Rights, or the Declaration of Independence; all comprise the bulwarks of one's liberties, rights, and blessings. God's covenant with Abraham represented Israel's rights and liberties. In doing so, we bring the spiritual nature of God's covenant into the natural and more practical truth to arrive at these terms of power. We use terms such as declaration, self-evidence, and unalienable, which apply perfectly to God's covenant with Israel.

First Term: Declaration

The first term, *declaration*, undergirds the covenant and explains how God creates everything and anything. When God created the earth, He declared it to be. He declared that the waters teem with every living thing and teemed with living things of all kinds. God declares something to be, and the manufacturing process begins and ends in one breath.

Declaration can also mean a divine utterance that is often delivered to man. For instance, when the Israelites sought the direction of Adonai through the *Urim* and *Thummim* and the *Ephod* of the high priest (1 Samuel 23:9; 30:7-8; 2 Samuel 28:6 1 Kings 6:16). Declaration can often be found in the King James Version to mean *saith*.

In the context of our study, *declaration* establishes nothing less than God's closeness to His people through promises that He has declared. It is made up of declarations, as in Isaiah 56:8 (NIV), *"The Sovereign Lord declares—he who gathers the exiles of Israel: 'I will gather still others to them besides those already gathered.'"*

God declared what He would do, and then He did it—He saved them. No foreign god had ever done this before. God declared:

> *You are my witnesses and my servants, chosen to know and to believe me and to understand that I alone am God. There is no other God; there never was and never will be. I am the Lord, and there is no other Savior. Whenever you have thrown away your idols, I have shown you my*

power. With one word I have saved you. You have seen me do it; you are my witnesses that it is true. From eternity to eternity, I am God. No one can oppose what I do (Isaiah 43:10-13 TLB).

Isaiah portrays almost a scene in a present-day courtroom where God is testifying and *declaring* before Heaven and earth against His people, which can also reveal His closeness to His people. God said, *"Hear me you heavens! Listen, earth! For the Lord has spoken: 'I reared children and brought them up, but they have rebelled against me'"* (Isaiah 1:2 NIV). And again, Isaiah states in 56:8 (NIV), *"The Sovereign Lord declares—he who gathers the exiles of Israel: 'I will gather still others to them besides those already gathered.'"*

The following words from two Psalms are important: His name is declared in Zion and His praise in Jerusalem, and the people of the world assemble to worship the Lord (see Psalm 102:21-22). Also, these well-known words, *"The Lord shall bless thee out of Zion, and thou shalt see the good of Jerusalem all the days of their life. Yea, thou shalt see thy children's children, and peace upon Israel"* (Psalm 128:5-6 KJV). Forty-five other passages are found in the Psalms alone like this showing God's love for His people.

In more than 400 places in Scripture, there is declaration upon declaration, precept upon precept, which establishes God's unchangeable devotion to the Jewish people and the land of Israel.

To conclude, all attempts to exterminate the Jews will fail because the Great I Am has *"declared he will set you* [Israel] *in praise, fame, and honor high above all the nations that he has made and that you will be a people holy to the Lord your God, as he promised"* (Deuteronomy 26:19 NIV).

Finally, consider the words of Isaiah:

> *People of Zion, who live in Jerusalem, you will weep no more. How gracious he will be when you cry for help! As soon as he hears, he will answer you* (Isaiah 30:19 NIV).
>
> *Listen! Your watchmen lift their voices; together they shout for joy. When the Lord returns to Zion, they will see it with their own eyes* (Isaiah 52:8 NIV).

Second Term: Self-Evidence

The second term, *self-evidence,* defines its own truth. Benjamin Franklin said, [Self-evidence is] "found through reason and is free from the Yoke of required proof of a legal theory."[1] He is speaking about our natural and individual rights founded upon natural law principles.

With this understanding, no one needs to provide evidence of their individual rights because our rights are *self-evident.* Today, Israel living in the Promised Land is self-evident of God's covenant with Abraham.

In the context of our study, self-evidence can be seen in the millions of believers who visit the Holy Land each year. God's covenant with the Jews, and the land of Israel, drives them there. To them, God's heart and plan for the Jewish people are *self-evident.*

Since 1948, Israel's independence, her *self-evidence,* has been before the world; the Jewish people have miraculously returned following thousands of years of wandering throughout the nations. This is *self-evidence* in its best light! One can only concede by the law of *self-evidence* that God has called the Jewish people, and Israel, to endure as the *apple of His eye.*

Third Term: Unalienable

The third term is *unalienable,* defined in Merriam-Webster Dictionary as rights "Impossible to take away or give up." In other words, no person has the power to trade or barter away the rights that our Creator endowed.

Regarding the Promised Land, we look back to one of the oldest understandings of unalienable English Common Law,[2] of which the United States and most commonwealth countries are heirs. It states, "Land cannot be given away, sold, or granted to another...the land can only be inherited. Thus it moves from one generation to the next."[3] Here we come very close to God's intention when He covenanted with Abraham and his heirs.

THOMAS JEFFERSON

When Thomas Jefferson, one of the founders of America, crafted the Declaration of Independence, he used the word *unalienable.*[4] But this put him at immediate odds with the Declaration Committee.

To understand why, we return to the original definition of *unalienable* because its meaning has changed from 300 years ago. Today, both words virtually mean the same, but in colonial days they meant the opposite.

Originally, *inalienable* rights meant, "incapable of being alienated, surrendered, or transferred, which allowed one to sell their rights, trade them, or even barter for them. Imagine how unstable our rights would be today.

The Declaration Committee immediately determined that if God our Creator endowed these rights to man, how can any one person or entity take away, give away, or even sell away what their Creator gave? Thankfully, the Declaration Committee immediately changed the wording to *unalienable* to guard people's rights forever.

ISRAEL'S UNALIENABLE RIGHTS

Applying what we have studied, unalienable rights define Israel's rights and position in the land. This means that she holds no lien or title to the land. Therefore, she has no right to sell or barter for them. It is God's tenant contract with the Jewish people.

This does not lessen the bond between Israel and God. This so-called tenant contract with the Jewish people qualifies Israel as the indisputable chosen stewards of the Promised Land; this is based upon their *unalienable* rights to God's vineyard.

Again, these words, *"The land must never be sold on a permanent basis, for the land belongs to me. You are only foreigners and tenant farmers working for me"* (Leviticus 25:23 NLT).

The famous thirteenth century exegete and biblical scholar Moses Nachmanides interprets the phrase, *"For the land is mine"* in Leviticus 25:23: "Here God is speaking to Israel through Moses: "You are but strangers' residents with me."

Two other translations convey the same idea, *"The land must not be sold permanently because the land is mine and you reside in my land as foreigners and strangers"* (NIV). The Living Bible says, *"And remember, the land is mine, so you may not sell it permanently. You are merely my tenants and sharecroppers!"*

In conclusion, no one can own the Holy Land other than God. He holds the *unalienable* rights, and Israel holds the *inalienable* rights. Further, no nation on earth has any rights to it. So when the United States pressures Israel to divide the land, God's *unalienable* rights as the landowner and Israel's *inalienable* rights as "the" *chosen stewards* are violated. This explosive mix will never turn out well for a nation. Consider this simple parable for illustration:

> A landowner was going on a long journey. He gave charge of his vineyard and his home to his servants to occupy, care for, and protect. Since the landowner had unalienable rights, he had the power and authority to confer this exclusive right to his tenants. In turn, the servants received the inalienable rights, their exclusive right to take possession of the vineyard.
>
> Others heard that the landowner was away on a long journey, and they began to pressure the ser-

vants to share the owner's vineyard. They began to overrun the borders; they offered to buy some of the land and offered to trade for the land. But the servants only possessed the *inalienable* rights and had no authority to do so.

Of course, hostility arose between the legal tenants and the others who wanted a portion of the landowner's vineyard. They did not realize that wanting claim to the land with equal status as the legal tenants violated both the landowner's *unalienable* rights and the servant's *inalienable* rights. The only way this could be settled was for the landowner to return.

SECOND PRINCIPLE OF ZION: GOD'S ENFORCEMENT OF HIS COVENANT

As the judiciary branch of the US safeguards our founders' documents, God safeguards His covenants. Natural events and/or spiritual principalities will be mobilized to do so.

Throughout biblical and church history, God intervened when humankind defied His laws. No principle is clearer regarding the Jewish people than Genesis 12:3 (NIV): *"I will bless those who bless you, and whoever curses you I will curse, and all peoples on earth will be blessed through you."* What does it mean to be blessed? And what does it mean to be cursed? Genesis 12:3 is a *conditional directive* from God that can be said of no other nation and people.

Based upon this promise and assurance from God, the land of Israel, as well as the Jew, sits upon an axis of cause and effect; God declares warnings or blessings to the world based upon their treatment of the Jew and the land of Israel; those that bless the Jew seem to be blessed, and those that curse the Jew seem to be cursed.

As extraordinary as this is, rarely has the world considered the Jews an extraordinary nation or people. Despite this, deep within the Jewish psyche is the awareness that they are a people chosen by the Almighty God.

ZECHARIAH'S LEGACY

One way to illustrate the Genesis 12:3 principle is to turn to the first three chapters of Zechariah. The prophet receives an extraordinary vision of the Babylonian captivity of the Jewish people. This vision occurs in Heaven, but the events occur on earth. (Please read Zechariah 1–3 to capture the entire scene.)

Horses of varied colors leave Heaven as their riders go on assignment to survey the disposition of the nations while the Jews are in seventy years of punishment in Babylon. These horses and riders were real invisible agencies that often let go of the glories of Heaven to complete an assignment.

In this particular case, the second person of the Godhead, Yeshua Himself, is leading them. He was the One the prophet saw by night riding a red horse and accompanied by other riders on speckled and white horses. Red is a sign of war and points to a disposition of anger.

Furthermore, when the Father sends His firstborn Son to do something, you know it is important! Who were they?

"These are they whom the Lord hath sent to walk to and fro through the earth" (Zechariah 1:10 KJV).

Throughout this passage, the Man standing amid the myrtle trees is the Angel of the Lord and the Man riding upon the red horse.

In Isaiah chapter 6, His identity is revealed as the Branch. Immediately, we know it is the Son since many passages also refer to the Son as the Branch: Zechariah 6:12; Jeremiah 33:15, 23:5; Isaiah 11:1, 4:2.

The Talmud also confirms that He is the second Person of the Godhead: "This Man can refer to none but the Holy One, blessed be he. He, as it is written, the Lord is a man of war" (Sanhedrin 93a).

As this scouting team returns from earth to give their report, God utters these words: *"I am very jealous for Jerusalem and Zion, and I am very angry with the nations that feel secure. I was only a little angry, but they went too far with the punishment"* (Zechariah 1:14-15 NIV). Babylon was certainly chosen to punish and discipline Israel, but they were *never* to exact unusual cruelty and go beyond what they had been commissioned to do (see Jeremiah chapters 27 and 28).

The phrase noted in Zechariah, *"nations that feel secure"* connotes arrogance. God takes notice of arrogant nations and their attitude toward the Jewish people. This passage establishes a timeless truth—when the Jewish people suffer at the hands of the nations, God is not only angered, but consequences also come to those nations.

I have often wondered if similar missions left Heaven during the Holocaust. How many nations, as the United States, lived feeling secure and at ease (arrogance) while 6 million Jewish were being killed? How many leaders, both in the United States and worldwide, have sought to divide the land of Israel in exchange for a Palestinian state and its consequences?

THIRD PRINCIPLE OF ZION: THE ANGEL OF THE LORD

John 1:1-2 states that Yeshua was the Word, and the Word was with God and was God. Therefore, His activity stretches into the dateless past, the spiritual, and the natural realm. Further, He has come to earth several times as the Angel of the Lord.

The Angel of the Lord appeared to Joshua as the commander of the army of the Lord with His sword drawn in His hand (Joshua 5:13-15). He appeared to John in Revelation 6:2, with a bow and crown; in Revelation 19:9-10 when He accepted Joshua's prostrate worship. He is seen when He found Hagar near a spring in Genesis 16:7. He also wrestled with Jacob in Genesis 32:30. Jacob records that he saw God face-to-face.

In Hosea in 12:4, the Angel of the Lord is mentioned, and again in Daniel 3:25. The Angel of the Lord was the fourth Man in the furnace, described as the "Son of God" (NKJV). Judges 2:1 mentions the Angel of the Lord as the One who brought the Israelites out of Egypt and spoke to the Israelites in verse 4. He is the One who sat under the tree in Ophrah in Judges 6:11 and received sacrifices and worship in Judges 13:20.

Again and again, Moses mentions the Angel of the Lord—seventeen times in the New Testament and sixty-two times in the Old Testament (NKJV). In Exodus 32:34, this angel had the power to forgive sins. Therefore, He was none other than the second Person of the divine Godhead appearing in His preincarnate state.

In the Talmud, the Angel of the Lord is compared with the Messiah because it states, "He spent part of his existence incarnated on Earth" (Sanhedrin 35a). He is called Metator, meaning the defender of the rights of Israel. His numerical value is that of the *Almighty*, and His name is *Metatron,* which is derived from *Metathronos,* "He whom God enthrones."

THE ACCUSER STEPS FORWARD

As we return to Zechariah's vision in Zechariah 3:1-5, Joshua or Yehoshua represents Israel in this most extraordinary scene. They stand before the Lord God Himself with satan present as the accuser of the brethren; this is the only such account in the Bible.

In this vision, satan steps into the representative place of power and deity, which is the right side. We must take a moment to review this extraordinary scene:

> Then he showed me Joshua the high priest standing before the angel of the Lord, and Satan standing at his right side to accuse him. The Lord said to Satan, "The Lord rebuke

*you, Satan! The Lord, who has chosen Jerusa-
lem, rebuke you! Is not this man a burning stick
snatched from the fire?"* (Zechariah 3:1-2 NIV)

The right side that satan takes is always connected with
the place of honor, power, and majesty (Psalm 16:11, 110:5,
118:16; Exodus 15:6). Always the right was reserved for the
Son (Luke 20:42; Acts 2:25; Romans 8:34). Satan is always
seeking to usurp the authority of the Father and is forever
craving the position of deity since his fall.

When we see "the" Man (Messiah) standing among
His people, symbolized by a lowly myrtle tree, He reveals
Himself as the *living eternal Guardian* and *Intercessor* over
Israel (see Zechariah 1:13; Hebrews 7:25). Though great suf-
fering will come upon the Jewish people in the latter days,
satan's plan to destroy them will fail.

The enduring message of Zechariah is that the Son of God
has long been active on Zion's behalf, even before 2,000 years
ago. Soon, the Son will return as the host's Captain and ride
a white horse as the One faithful and true (Revelation 19).

Again and again God's long-held devotion to Zion is
established, and His concern for the Gentile's treatment of
the Jew is also clear.

FOURTH PRINCIPLE OF ZION: A PEOPLE FASHIONED FOR SUCCESS

*And thou say in thine heart, My power and the
might of mine hand hath gotten me this wealth.
But thou shalt remember the Lord thy God: for*

> *it is he that giveth thee power to get wealth, that he may establish his covenant which he swore unto thy fathers, as it is this day* (Deuteronomy 8:17-18 KJV).

History reveals that the Jew possesses a rare ability to emerge from tyranny and social injustice. Tenacity defines them. Few nations can match their successes, yet they rise out of the most insufferable circumstances. Their inexorable drive to survive is only by divine providence.

Linked to it are the words of Moses to the Israelites in the context of the Abrahamic covenant. From Young's Literal Translation, *"...He it [is] who is giving to thee power to make wealth, to establish His covenant which He hath sworn to thy fathers as [at] this day"* (Deuteronomy 8:18).

Literally, again and again, the Jew affirms God's covenant with them. Imagine if they had not survived and if Israel had been destroyed. Wouldn't our entire future be uncertain? If only one declaration and promise—let alone the multitude of promises and declarations over Israel would fail—God's entire word is rendered impotent.

What is clear by any observer of history, the Jew has been wired for survival and succession from one generation to the next. But were these endowments given also to testify to the nations of His covenant people? Finally, are the Jewish people a forthcoming kingdom community and nation that will complete the Kingdom to come?

The answer to these questions is, of course, yes. And most important, the nations were to marvel at this epic journey of the Jew and wonder how they miraculously survived from generation to generation. This can only be attributed to divine providence.

What Have the Jews Accomplished?

Historically, Jews have become vital assets and contributors wherever they have settled. This is in spite of the fact that the Jewish population is less than 1 percent of the world's population. In other words, more than 99 percent of the world is non-Jewish. And in the words of the Torah, Israel is "the fewest and weakest of all the nations" (see Deuteronomy 7:7).

Consider that the World Bank no longer classifies Israel as a developing country; Israel ranks as a high-income economy and is identified as one of the most global emerging markets by the foreign policy magazine *Globalization Index.*

Israel has ranked third in citizens holding university degrees, after the United States and Holland. Israel has the fourth largest air force in the world after the US, Russia, and China. It is the only progressive and tolerant self-government compared to the countries surrounding her.

Further, more new companies were produced in Israel, and more Israeli companies are listed on the NASDAQ stock exchange for small promising companies than the combined countries just mentioned. Former Google CEO and Chairman Eric Schmidt said that Israel is the best place in the world for entrepreneurs after the United States. Morgan Stanley Capital International decided to upgrade Israel from an emerging market to a developed market in 2010.

Steven Balmer, Microsoft's former Chief Executive officer, has called Microsoft an Israeli company as much as an American company because of all the Microsoft teams working in Israel. Israel has eight universities and twenty-seven colleges, four are among the top one hundred fifty worldwide universities, and seven are in the top one hundred Asia Pacific universities.

From a recent book titled *Start-Up Nation,* by Dan Senor and Saul Singer, addresses what is called the trillion-dollar question:

> How is Israel, a country of just over 7.5 million, surrounded by enemies bent on their demise, producing more start-up companies than large, peaceful nations like Canada, Japan, China, India, and the UK? With the savvy of foreign policy insiders, Senor and Singer examine Israeli culture and government to reveal the secrets behind the world's first-ever "start-up nation." As countries across the globe restart their own economies and as businesses try to re-energize their entrepreneurial spirit, we can all look to Israel for some impressive, surprising clues.[5]

MIRACULOUS ISRAEL ARISES

The scale of achievements in a country less than the size of New Jersey (roughly 8,850 square miles) is astounding! Ernest Van Den Haag, well-known social critic, public policy professor, and writer for the National Review, said this of the Jews, "They have recorded more of [history], shaped more of it, originated and developed more of it, and suffered more for it than any other people, yet Jews have changed history."[6]

When anyone reviews the history of Jewish achievements, they cannot but sense the supernatural in it, which brings us back to God's blessings to Abraham and his seed. Winston Churchill said, "Some people like the Jews, and some do not. But no thoughtful man can deny that they are, beyond any question, the most formidable and remarkable race which has appeared in the world."

EXAMPLES OF REMARKABLE ABILITIES

Medicine

- Dr. Selman Abraham Waksman coined the term *antibiotics.*

- Dr. Paul "Magic Bullet" Ehrlich won the Nobel Prize in 1908 for curing syphilis.

- Dr. Abraham Jacobi is known as America's father of pediatrics.

- Dr. Simon Baruch performed the first successful operation for appendicitis.

- Casimir Funk, a Polish Jew, pioneered a new field of medical research and coined the word *vitamins.*

Business and Finance

- Haym Salomon and Isaac Moses created the first modern banking institution.

- Jews created the first department stores: Altman's, Gimbels, Kaufmanns, Lazarus's, Magnins, Mays, and Strauss that all became leaders of major department stores.

- Julius Rosenwald revolutionized the way Americans purchased goods by improving Sears Roebuck's mail-order merchandising.

- Hart, Schaffner, Marx, Kuppenheimer, and Levi Strauss became household names in men's clothing.

- Isidor and Nathan Straus, Abraham & Strauss, owned Macy's, the world's largest department store.

- Armand Hammer (Arm & Hammer) was a physician and businessman who originated the largest trade between the US and Russia.

- Louis de Santangel was the financier who provided the funds for Columbus's voyage to America.

- Mark Zuckerberg created Facebook which revolutionized social media.

Entertainment

- Samuel Goldwyn and Louis B. Mayer (MGM) produced the first full-length sound picture, *The Jazz Singer*.

- European Jews are the founders of all the Hollywood studios.

- Adolph Zukor built the first theater used to show motion pictures.

- George and Ira Gershwin and Irving Berlin are three of the most prolific composers of the twentieth century.

- Sherry Lansing of Paramount became the first woman president of a major Hollywood studio.

- Steven Spielberg is the most successful film-maker since the advent of film.

Famous Jewish Actors and Musicians

- Henry Winkler (the Fonzie) / Charlie Chaplin / Clark Gable / Woody Allen / Jeff Bridges / James Brolin / Mel Brooks / George Burns / Ben Stiller / Harrison Ford / Art Garfunkel / Carly Simon / Phil Silvers /William Shatner / Peter Sellers / Jerry Seinfeld / Adam Sandler / Edward G. Robinson / Don Rickles / Leonard Nimoy / Marilyn Monroe / Zero Mostel / Bette Midler / Walter Matthau / Jackie Mason / Marx Brothers / Barry Manilow / Jerry Lewis / Richard Dreyfus / Billy Crystal / Bob Dylan / Barbra Streisand / Soupy Sales / The Three Stooges / Lauren Bacall / Jack Benny

Inventions

- Theodore Judah was chief architect and engineer of the first American transcontinental railroad.

- In 1909, four Jews were among the sixty multi-cultural signers of the Call to the National Action, which resulted in the creation of the NAACP.

- In 1910, Louis Blaustein and his son opened the first gas station, eventually founding Amoco Oil.

- In 1918, Max Goldberg opened the first commercial parking lot, located in Detroit.

- Emil Berliner developed the modern-day phonograph. The machine he patented was called the gramophone. Berliner made possible the modern record industry. The Victor Talking Machine Company, now known as RCA, absorbed his company.

- A Jew invented the first printing press in 1563 in Asia.

- Israel produces more scientific papers, has the highest number of scientists and technicians, the highest number of PhDs, and the highest number of physicians per capita than any other nation in the world by a large margin.

- More Israeli patents are registered by Israelis than Russian, India, and China.

Telecommunications

- A Jewish person in the Israeli branch of Motorola developed the cell phone.

- Jewish people developed most of the Windows NT and XP operating systems.

- A Jewish person at Intel Corporation designed the Pentium MMX chip technology.

- Jewish people in Israel developed, designed, and produced the Pentium 4 microprocessor and the Centrino processor.

- Instant Messenger. The so-called "original instant messenger" was none other than ICQ, a free-to-download app developed in 1996 by Israeli Internet company Mirabilis.

- USB Drive: An Israeli patent paved the way for one of the world's most common everyday items, the portable USB memory drive.

- The Intel 8088 microprocessor that powered the first IBM PC build, which credited with kick-starting the PC revolution.

Exploration and Art

- A Jewish person concluded before all others that the world was round (Judah Cresques, better known as Map Jew).

- The first man to set foot in the New World was not Columbus but his Jewish interpreter, Luis de Torres (born Yosef ben HaLevi HaIvri).

- Jewish financier Haym Salomon supported the American Revolution.

- Jewish composer Irving Berlin composed the song "God Bless America."

- Jewish artist Marc Chagall's stained-glass "peace window" adorns a wall in the United Nations building.

- Jewish poet Emma Lazarus wrote the inscription on the Statue of Liberty: "Give me your tired...your poor...your huddled masses."

Economics

- Israel, the 100th smallest country, with 1/1000th of the world's population, has a $100 billion economy that is larger than all of its immediate neighbors combined.

- Israel has the highest ratio of university degrees and produces more scientific papers per capita than any other nation.

- Israel has the highest average living standards in the Middle East.

- Twenty-four percent of Israel's workforce holds university degrees, ranking third in the industrialized world after the United States and the Netherlands.

- Israel is the only country that entered the twenty-first century with a net gain in its number of trees, a remarkable achievement considering its desert land.

Food and Ice Cream

- Ben & Jerry's ice cream was founded in 1977 by Ben Cohen and Jerry Greenfield with $12,000; now worth about $500 million.

- Tom Carvel, of Greek Jewish descent, who arrived in New York in 1910, founded Carvel Ice Cream.

- Born in Williamsburg, David Mintz created Tofutti, the world-famous dairy-free ice cream.

- Hebrew National was founded by Isadore Pinckowitz, a Romanian immigrant butcher who began his career peddling meat from the back of a horse-drawn wagon. Pinckowitz (later known as Isidore Pines) bought the Hebrew National Kosher Sausage Factory in 1928.

- Reuben and Rose Mattus, Polish Jews, founded Haagen-Dazs.

- William Rosenberg was an American entrepreneur who founded the Dunkin Donuts franchise in 1950 in Quincy, Massachusetts.

Spiritually and Prophetically

- God chose the Jewish people to be head of the nations (Deuteronomy 28:13,44).

- God chose the Jewish people to transmit the Word of God to future generations (Romans 3:1-2).

- God chose the Jewish people for an end-time worldwide revival (Revelation 7:1-14).

- The Jewish people hold the key to the second coming (Matthew 23:39; Hosea 5:15).

- The Jewish people will determine who enters the Messianic kingdom by the nations' treatment of them during Jacob's Trouble or the Great Tribulation (Matthew 25).

- The Jewish people will confer upon the Gentiles the tribe of their choosing in the coming age (Ezekiel 47:23).

- The Jewish people were chosen to bring the Messiah to the world.

- The Jewish people were chosen to be first to receive the infilling the Holy Spirit (Acts 1 and 2).

- Israel is the only Jewish state whose people returned to their native land 2,000 years after forced exile.

FIFTH PRINCIPLE OF ZION— FOR HIS NAME'S SAKE

Unlike man, God's actions always align with His glory and the sanctity of His Name, setting Him apart from humanity. The restoration of Israel and the Jewish people are purposefully orchestrated for His glory and name's sake. This is a truism that the future glory of Zion has always been dependent upon: *"For Zion's sake will I not hold my peace, and for Jerusalem's sake I will not rest, until the righteousness thereof go forth as brightness, and the salvation thereof as a lamp that burneth"* (Isaiah 62:1 KJV).

For His name's sake, Heaven and earth will be mobilized. He saved His people and manifested His might and power to deliver them. Psalm 106:8 (NIV) states, *"He saved them for his name's sake to make his mighty power known."* From the book of Ezekiel 20:22 (KJV), *"Nevertheless I withdrew mine hand, and wrought for my name's sake that it should not be polluted in the sight of the heathen, in whose sight I brought them forth."*

The prophet Ezekiel provides an abundance of Scripture pointing to the importance of upholding God's holy name. Ezekiel 39:7 (NIV) states, *"I will make known my holy name among my people Israel. I will no longer let my holy name be profaned, and the nations will know that I, the Lord am the Holy One in Israel."*

Then from Ezekiel 39:25 (NIV), *"Therefore this is what the Sovereign Lord says: I will now restore the fortunes of Jacob and will have compassion on all the people of Israel, and I will be zealous for my holy name."*

Finally, consider the following:

> *Therefore say to the Israelites, "This is what the Sovereign Lord says: It is not for your sake, people of Israel, that I am going to do these things, but for the sake of my holy name, which you have profaned among the nations where you have gone. I will show the holiness of my great name, which has been profaned among*

the nations, the name you have profaned among them. Then the nations will know that I am the Lord, declares the Sovereign Lord, when I am proved holy through you before their eyes" (Ezekiel 36:22-23 NIV).

HIS NAME'S SAKE: MA'AN

The word in Hebrew for *sake* is *ma'an* and most often it is why God intervenes in the affairs of man. If, in some way, Israel could be destroyed, God's name would collapse, and His promises would be powerless.

Just consider some of the future events that rely upon God's promises for Israel being upheld, as well as these words: *"This is what the Lord says: 'Only if the heavens above can be measured and the foundations of the earth below be searched out will I reject all the descendants of Israel because of all they have done'"* (Jeremiah 31:37 NIV).

- Where would King Yeshua establish His temple? (Zechariah 14:8-9)

- How would the nations gather in Jerusalem to worship the Lord during the Feast of Tabernacles? (Zechariah 14:16)

- How would Israel become the head of the nations? (Deuteronomy 8:13)

- Where would the universal world government of the greater Son of David be established and how? (2 Chronicles 6:16)

- Who will judge the poor of the people? Where would judgment take place? (Psalm 72:4; Isaiah 11:4; Psalm 106:8-12)

- When would the nations be blessed by Him as the sun and moon endure, throughout all generations as spoken in (Psalm 72:17-18)

- How would the righteous flourish and the abundance of peace endure as the moon endured? (Daniel 7:10; Matthew 26:53; Hebrews 12:22)

- What would be made of His glorious name and promises? (Habakkuk 2:14)

In conclusion, humans cannot render the Scriptures impotent. Let these final words of Jeremiah echo through our hearts:

> *This is what the Lord says, "If you can break my covenant with the day and my covenant with the night so that day and night no longer come at their appointed time, then my covenant with David, my servant—and my covenant with the Levites who are priests ministering before me—can be broken and David will no longer have a descendant to reign on his throne. I will make the descendants of David my servant and the Levites who minister before me as countless as the stars of the sky and as measureless as the sand on the seashore"* (Jeremiah 33:20-22 NIV).

5

UNLOCKING ISRAEL'S ELECTION

UNLOCKING ISRAEL'S ELECTION[1] (OR WHAT IT MEANS TO be the Chosen People), takes us to the attitudes and mindsets of the early church fathers, and to understand how the church severed the Jewish root, and how Jewish election became a Gentile orientation.

Certainly, in the first century, the believers were mainly Jewish people who understood their *theological* and *hierological* right as Jews to be Israel; their distinction and place in the family were well understood.

But their identity and place began to erode in church thinking. One of the most sinister and damaging was when the Jewish people were blamed for Yeshua's death. For generations, the Jewish people have been vilified as Christ-killers. Even today, thousands of years later, streams within Christianity see the Jews as Christ-killers.

While Yeshua's death was timely according to Scripture, can anyone be blamed for it? No hefty Roman soldier wrestled Him to the ground; no soldiers forcefully held Him down while they drove the nails through His hands and feet. Yeshua laid down His life willingly while bearing the weight of the cross upon His own shoulders. His suffering took place exactly as it was foretold.

When He stated, *"Father, forgive them, for they do not know what they are doing"* (Luke 23:34 NIV), He pointed out that every person—Jew, Roman, and Greek—played a providential role in God's divine plan for humankind. Labeling Jews as Christ-killers came from a dark conspiracy of satan that vilified them for centuries.

Consider the following words:

> *Surely he took up our pain and bore our suffering, yet we considered him punished by God, stricken by him, and afflicted. But he was pierced for our transgressions, he was crushed for our iniquities; the punishment that brought us peace was on him, and by his wounds we are healed. We all, like sheep, have gone astray, each of us has turned to our own way; and the Lord has laid on him the iniquity of us all. He was oppressed and afflicted, yet he did not open his mouth; he was led like a lamb to the slaughter, and as a sheep before its shearers is silent, so he did not open his mouth. By oppression and judgment he was taken away. Yet who*

of his generation protested? For he was cut off from the land of the living; for the transgression of my people he was punished. He was assigned a grave with the wicked, and with the rich in his death, though he had done no violence, nor was any deceit in his mouth. Yet it was the Lord's will to crush him and cause him to suffer, and though the Lord makes his life an offering for sin, he will see his offspring and prolong his days, and the will of the Lord will prosper in his hand (Isaiah 53:4-10 NIV).

SECOND MISUNDERSTANDING

Another misunderstanding occurred in the year 70 when the Roman army led by Titus destroyed the Temple and sacked Jerusalem (the spiritual center of Judaism at the time). Early church fathers viewed it as damnatory evidence that God permanently cut off the Jewish people and that He no longer considered them His covenant people.

Church fathers were convinced that God was preparing the world for a new religion, Christianity. From this new religion, a new spiritual Israel, the church, would be born, and a new covenant people, the Gentile, would replace the old covenant people, the Jews. They didn't understand the distinction between the generation being judged in Matthew chapters 12, 16, and 23 and the Jewish people as a whole.

In those passages, Yeshua condemns that generation that committed the unpardonable sin (Mathew 12). He said that they *"shut the door of the kingdom of heaven in people's faces"*

(Matthew 23:13 NIV). Then the chapters leading up to chapter 24 culminate in a climactic conversation with His disciples concerning this great judgment that would come in the year 70 by the Romans. He states, *"'Do you see all these things' he asked. 'Truly I tell you, not one stone here will be left on another; every one will be thrown down'"* (Matthew 24:2 NIV). Again, Yeshua was not casting judgment on the Jewish people as a whole, but on the generation that existed that day.

THE ATMOSPHERE CHANGES

Repeatedly, we must stress an increasing anti-Jewish atmosphere that influenced the early church fathers. As the Jewish root was cut for a new Roman root, or essentially an entirely new tree, to replace the original olive tree, the idea of Jewish election ceased in the minds of generations forward.

The early church began to seek uniformity and independence apart from Judaism, believing that she had now *replaced, fulfilled,* and *completed* the promises given exclusively to the Jews. Not only did the church believe it, she reveled in it. One individual, such as Justin Martyr, viewed the church as the *new true spiritual Israel.*

In the epistle of Barnabas, Christians are urged to assume their role as the new Israel. Cyprian, a Catholic saint who died in the year 258, was bishop of Carthage and an important writer of his day. He insisted that because Jews have forsaken the Lord and profaned the Holy One of Israel, Christians are now permitted to call God "Our Father" since He has become ours and ceased to be theirs—the Jews.[2]

SUPERSESSIONISM AND REPLACEMENT THEOLOGY EMERGES

Following in the patterns mentioned, a deceptive line of thinking developed that created a well-known theology called "replacement theology," or what is known as "supersessionism," also, "fulfillment theology" or even "displacement theology." All carry the idea that comes from the Latin words *super* (on-upon) and *sedere* (to sit) as one sits on the chair of another person or a person displaces another person. In this case, the Gentile sits in the chair of the Jew, and the church takes the place of a new spiritual Israel.

The enemy's intrusion into the early New Covenant community would bury the truth about the Jewish election and calling for generations. Following this, the early church replaced the synagogue. The New Testament replaced the Old Testament, Sunday replaced Saturday, and the Gentile Christian replaced the Jew. Christian holidays and holy days replaced the biblical feasts.

The Effect on the Kingdom

The understanding of the Kingdom underwent a dramatic transformation, discussed extensively in a subsequent chapter, and shifted entirely toward a spiritual and abstract notion. The concept of a tangible government, in which the Jewish people would fulfill their chosen status, was lost. Consequently, the Jews lost their unique identity and distinct calling, gradually becoming oriented toward the Gentiles. This shift in perspective fostered generations inclined toward anti-Semitism.

As a result, the promises of blessing and restoration originally intended for the Jewish people were conveniently reassigned to the church. Conversely, the Scriptures depicting judgment and wrath remained squarely attributed to the Jewish people.

In summary, a system of thinking and belief emerged that fueled prejudice against Jews, while the concept of the Kingdom took shape without any Jewish involvement.

True Jewish Calling

To fully comprehend Jewish election and calling, we begin with the simple principle of distinction, because God has long made distinctions in everything He does.

Consider that our regular days are distinct from the Sabbath. Light is distinct from darkness, common months from holy months, and common years from holy years (Sabbatical years). Nature is wrought with creative distinction. Races, languages, and geographies are all born in the creative crucible of distinction.

Few subjects carry as much weight as the family of God and the differentiation between His first, and second-born, namely the Jew and the Gentile. However, instead of appreciating the significance of this distinction, it has consistently posed a stumbling block throughout the history of the Christian church, persisting even in our contemporary times.

To go deeper, we turn to the *Song of Moses, Shirat Haazinu*as, as it begins with Jewish election. God states, *"Remember the days of old, consider the years of many generations. ...When the Most High divided their inheritance to the* nations.... *For the Lord's portion is His people"* (Deuteronomy 32:7-9 NKJV).

This song also mentions God's favor toward Israel, saying, *"He found him in a desert land...He encircled, instructed, and kept him as the apple of His eye"* (Deuteronomy 32:10 NKJV).

The prophet Amos gives one more view of election: Jew and Gentile are two children who are equally loved. *"Are ye not as the children of Ethiopia unto me, O children of Israel?"* (Amos 9:7 KJV). A branch thought of election emerges here that states that all nations are fundamentally alike in the eyes of God because God is still the Creator of humankind.

Yet, God has selected Israel, as seen by the prophet Amos in these words, *"You only have I known of all the families of the earth: therefore I will punish you for all your iniquities"* (Amos 3:2 KJV).

From these words, divine selection is owed not to ethnic or national superiority. Neither does their election release them from punishment for their sins. This principle of distinction is not superiority, but the opposite. It is a calling and service to God.

DIVINE PROVIDENCE

Beloved, Jewish election is an eternal, divine selection made by our loving Abba Father, past, present, and future. As mentioned in Amos 3:2 (KJV), this divine providence signifies God's deliberate choice of the Jewish people. This was not based on their size or strength, but rather on their smallness and vulnerability, as stated in Deuteronomy 7:7.

By divine providence alone, God selected Israel and the Jewish people to be distinct from all nations. Consequently, based on historical, biblical, and prophetic accounts, no nation can substitute Israel in their unique position. The connection between election and chosen-ness is direct; they are inseparable.

The apostle Paul uses a different term in Romans 11:29 (NIV), *"God's gifts and his call are irrevocable."* This important relationship has long been underestimated, ignored, and misinterpreted, especially by *dispensational* and *reformed* theologians. Let us review this briefly for greater foundation.

- *Dispensationalists* believe that God has two programs in history, one for Israel and one for the church, and that the two groups are unrelated. Large parts of the church world still believe this.

- *Reformed* theologians believe that the promises made to Israel have been or will be fulfilled in the church and that God no longer has a special relationship with the nation of Israel. This is finally coming to light for what it truly is, re-placement theology. But many remain in this mindset.

John Calvin believed that "all Israel" pertained to all the redeemed, both Jews and Gentiles. If correct, Paul is saying that when a full number of people are saved in the future, all of Israel will be saved because the two are synonymous.

Calvin's view ignores that Paul speaks of Israel and the Gentiles as two distinct groups. Here, the Jewish people experienced a hardening until the full number of Gentiles had been saved, and Israel would then turn from their unbelief and be saved. But this latter view wipes out the principle of distinction entirely. Still, Romans 11:26 teaches that God has not rejected His people, and so all Israel will be saved, as it is written.

Despite everything, Paul, in Romans 11:1-32, claims that while Israel's unbelief is purposeful, it is temporary. He always leans toward partial hardening rather than the historical Christian view of complete and permanent rejection where no chance of Jewish salvation exists. In verses 33-36, we immediately see Paul's understanding of God's wisdom and knowledge throughout the passage.

Stating it again, the church has assumed that a full hardening has taken place with little or no chance of a return for the Jew, and the Gentile have become the new heirs. A final question remains, however, what is chosen-ness?

A FINAL QUESTION: WHAT IS CHOSEN-NESS?

As we study Christian church history, the label of the "chosen people" has been a thorny experience for Jewish people, pricking them often. Jews have long thought it might be better for others to be the chosen people for a change.

Many have interpreted God's sovereign choice as a message from God that He loves the Jew more. But this needs to be corrected. The Jew is not loved more or less. The Jew carries no more grace than the Gentile. Both Jew and Gentile receive the same equal blessing of love and devotion of our Abba Father.

Ironically, the Jew is often subject to God's wrath in a double portion because of their divine calling. *"Speak comfort to Jerusalem, and cry out to her, that her warfare is ended, that her iniquity is pardoned; for she has received from the Lord's hand double for all her sins"* (Isaiah 40:2 NKJV).

JEWISH CALLING (ELECTION) AND DISTINCTION

To be chosen, as we have noted, means to be selected or elected, for a particular task and responsibility. In Exodus 19:5-6 (KJV), we discover first what the Jew was selected for: *"Now therefore, if ye will obey my voice indeed, and keep my covenant, then ye shall be a peculiar treasure unto me above all people: for all the earth is mine. And ye shall be unto me a kingdom of priests, and a holy nation...."* Isaiah writes in chapter 42:6 (NIV): *"...I will keep you and will make you to be a covenant for the people and a light for the Gentiles."*

The initial purpose of their calling was priestly in nature, aiming to spread the knowledge of the One True God among the nations and inspire universal recognition of the Almighty's sovereignty, thereby fostering a belief in Him.

The second calling pertained to leadership, as stated in Deuteronomy 15:6 (NIV): *"For the Lord your God will bless you as he has promised, and you will lend to many nations but will borrow from none. You will rule over many nations, but none will rule over you."* Furthermore, Deuteronomy 28:13 (NKJV) reinforces this notion, declaring, *"The Lord will make you the head and not the tail; you shall be above only, and not be beneath...."*

Certainly, since the Jewish people rejected their Messiah, all is not lost as Christian church thinking has leaned toward. The Jew remains at a launch pad, ready to fulfill what God has chosen for them. The following is an expansion of Jewish distinction.

SIX JEWISH DISTINCTIONS

The Jewish people have a distinct calling and relationship with God. No other nation and people were personally and directly chosen, covenanted with, and communicated to by God through the Abrahamic Covenant, Land Covenant, Davidic Covenant, and New Covenants (Genesis 12–17; Deuteronomy 29 and 30:1-10; 2 Samuel 7; 10–13; 1 Chronicles 17:11-14; Jeremiah 31:31-34). No other nation was given a specific land by God that He called His own and to which He would return. Hence, a people remain who can trace their history and occupation to a homeland that is more than three thousand years old (Genesis 15:18-21, 28:13; Exodus 23:31; Deuteronomy 1:8).

The Jewish people have a distinct history. No other nation or people has been so systematically and relentlessly pursued for destruction and persecution. No other nation is at the center of a relational drama with God unfolding from one chapter to the next. Israel is called in the Old Testament the "Wife of Jehovah" (Ezekiel 16:8; Hosea 2–5, 14–23; Isaiah 50:1, 54:1-8; Jeremiah 3:6-10; Ezekiel 16:35-43, 16:6).

The Jewish people have a distinct prophetic destiny. No other nation was given an irrevocable calling with clear and specific details. No other nation is essential to the return of the Lord and the completion of the Messianic Order (Romans 11:29; Matthew 8:18, 19:28, 23:37-39, 25:31-46; Luke 22:27-30; Jeremiah 39:9; Daniel 12:9-13; Isaiah 1:26; Ezekiel 45:8, Hosea 5:15; Zechariah 12:10).

The Jewish people have a distinct relationship to the nations. No other nation has been assigned to be a servant and priest to the nations. No other nation has been called to be the head of the nations in a future Kingdom under King Yeshua. Finally, no other nation was told by God that all other nations will be blessed if they bless them and cursed if they curse them (Isaiah 42:6; Genesis 12:3).

The Jewish people have a distinct identity. No other nation is called God's Firstborn Son, the Apple of His Eye, His Chosen People, Peculiar Treasure (Zechariah 2:8; Exodus 4:23; Deuteronomy 7:6; Psalm 135:4).

The Jewish people have a special agreement with God. The covenant of circumcision was a sign of the Abrahamic Covenant, which included the original promise to Abraham that all the nations of the earth would be blessed through him (Genesis 12:1-3). Over time, the Abrahamic Covenant included additional promises, such as the promise of the land of Israel to the descendants of Abraham (Genesis 15:18-21). The purpose of the sign of the covenant of circumcision was to set the descendants of Abraham apart from the other nations of the earth (Genesis 17; Acts 7:8). It was a physical symbol of the unique relationship between God and Abraham and his descendants.

6

THE BATTLE FOR ISRAEL AND THE MESSIANIC KINGDOM

IT HAS BECOME EVIDENT THAT ISRAEL'S REJECTION OF their Messiah does not signify a complete loss. Significant aspects of God's prophetic plan are yet to unfold.

Although God's promises to Israel remain unfulfilled, one of His purposes in allowing a delay in the fullness of those promises is to enable multiple opportunities for the inclusion of people from all nations in the blessing of salvation that He offers through His Son, Yeshua. For when the fullness of the Jewish people comes in, *all Israel is saved* (Romans 11:26) and a new era shall begin called the "Messianic Kingdom," or the "Restoration Age."

During this time, Yeshua will reign as King over all the earth from Jerusalem (Zechariah 14:9), and Israel will finally receive the fullness of God's promises. But this Restoration

Age is not only for Israel. It is also a time of blessing and salvation for all the nations. In fact, one of the main purposes of Israel's restoration is to be a blessing to the nations (Genesis 12:3). God desires for people from all nations to come to know Him and receive His salvation.

Throughout history, God has been extending His invitation to people from all nations to be part of His family. In the Old Testament, we see examples of non-Israelites who chose to follow and serve God, such as Rahab the Canaanite and Ruth the Moabite. In the New Testament, the Good News of salvation through Yeshua is preached to all nations, and people from every tribe, tongue, and nation are welcomed into God's Kingdom (Revelation 7:9).

God's plan is not to exclude any nation or people group from His blessings, but to include everyone who desires to come to Him. He is the God of love and mercy, not willing that any should perish, but that all should come to faith.

As documented in Romans 11, God's promises to Israel will be fulfilled in His own time and in His own way. Until then, Jews continue to come to faith, but also as many people as possible from all nations will come into a living relationship with Him through faith in Yeshua.

In light of this, the challenge for Gentile Christians today can be summarized in Paul's words from Romans 11:11 (NIV): *"Again I ask: Did they stumble so as to fall beyond recovery? Not at all! Rather, because of their transgression, salvation has come to the Gentiles to make Israel envious."*

This mandate places upon us an obligation not only to spread the Good News of Yeshua, but also to acknowledge and honor the distinct role that Israel continues to hold in God's prophetic blueprint. It requires us to bring the message of Yeshua to the Jewish people residing in Israel as well as those scattered across the Diaspora (Jewish communities worldwide).

THE KINGDOM

Yes, the Messianic Kingdom will indeed see the fulfillment of God's calling upon the Jewish people. The Scriptures are clear that during this time, the Jewish people will have a special role and position within God's government on earth. A fulness of His promises through the Jewish people will take hold, and the blessings of salvation will come to the whole world (John 4:22). This Messianic Kingdom will not be a time of exclusion or oppression for other nations, but a time of peace, justice, and harmony for all.

In Isaiah 11:6-9, it is described how the wolf will dwell with the lamb, the leopard will lie down with the young goat, and the lion will eat straw like the ox. This imagery symbolizes the restoration of creation and the restoration of relationships between all creation, including humans.

DAVID'S RULE

In Ezekiel 37:24-28, God promises that King David will be raised up to rule over a reunited Israel, and the Jewish people will be God's people forever. In Isaiah 2:3, it is prophesied that the law and the word of the Lord will go forth from

Jerusalem, indicating that Jerusalem will be the spiritual and political center of the world during this time.

Furthermore, in Zechariah 8:23, God says that in the Messianic Kingdom, ten men from every nation will grasp the garment of a Jewish man, saying, *"Let us go with you, for we have heard that God is with you."* This indicates that there will be a clear recognition and respect for the Jewish people and their special relationship with God.

Throughout our journey, the concept of "thy Kingdom come" has been a constant companion. But seeing the Messianic Kingdom with the chosen position of the Jewish people, is where we witness the undeniable and unchangeable calling upon the Jewish people in a future government on earth.

Furthermore, an unwavering battle continues to challenge God's envisioned Kingdom. Regrettably, there is a dearth of teachings concerning this Kingdom, despite its profound significance in relation to Israel's ultimate purpose and the factors contributing to their endurance. The following delves into this neglected subject: the roots of anti-Semitism and the historical campaigns to eradicate the Jewish people and Israel.

For this, we turn to the book of Isaiah in chapter 14:13-15, where the five "I wills" are recorded. They are the most notorious statements ever made by the adversary. There we discover his blinding intention to be worshiped on God's holy mount, the congregation of the North in Jerusalem, in a future order that will never be his.

In conclusion, the only judicious reason for anti-Semitism is here. And for the same, satan robbed the church of the truth about the Jewish election and the Kingdom to come. Isaiah 14:13-15 (NIV) records what satan stated in his heart:

"I will ascend to the heavens"—Here, Lucifer desired to occupy the highest heavens: penetrate the Kingdom of the infinite God and want the highest position. He saw himself exalted above all!

"I will raise my throne above the stars of God"—lucifer's position and service before God's throne were not enough here. He wanted final authority to make decisions about the angelic host (the stars of God). He wanted to rule over all the angels. Though God had made him an exalted angel, he was not content to shine as the "morning star"—he wanted to shine as the star of stars—one that would outshine all the other stars.

"I will set enthroned on the mount of assembly"—A millennial term that refers to the ultimate temple location in the Messianic Kingdom. He wants to be the center of worship upon the Temple Mount in the Millennial Temple. *"He stretched out what looked like a hand and took me by the hair of my head. The Spirit lifted me up between earth and heaven and in visions of God he took me to Jerusalem, to the entrance of the north gate of the inner court, where the idol that provokes to jealousy stood"* (Ezekiel 8:3 NIV).

"I will ascend above the tops of the clouds"—Here, clouds are often used in the Bible to speak of the glory of God (see Matthew 24:30; Acts 1:9; Revelation 1:7). Lucifer coveted God's glory for his own. He failed to acknowledge that his

glory and beauty all came from and was dependent upon God. In his sinful pride, lucifer wanted a glory that would impress and dazzle all creatures.

"I will make myself like the Most High"—Here, he wanted to be *equal* with God and to take God's place as possessor and ruler of all. He wanted to become a completely independent creature responsible to no one.

THE FUTURE KINGDOM

Despite satan's attempts to deprive the earth of God's plan, our future will be the incomparable vision of our Creator. But many believe that Heaven is our ultimate destination.

Yes, we will go to Heaven, praise God, but not for a limitless period. Our real future will be with our Messiah for 1,000 years in His Kingdom, and that very Kingdom will take us into the New Earth.

When we think about this future Kingdom, many think of it as purely ethereal, but in fact it will be both material, and spiritual. It will have a geography, people, and places to rule. Messiah's government will have branches of government. And something seldom considered is that corruptible people will inhabit the earth with the incorruptible.

Who are the incorruptible and corruptible?

The incorruptible ones are those who have been raptured and returned to co-reign with Messiah; the corruptible ones are those who have endured the tribulation, gave their life to Messiah, and have entered the Messianic Kingdom. Hence, the corruptible will dwell with the incorruptible; material and spiritual (1 Corinthians 15:53; 1 Peter 1:23).

In actuality, the corruptible ones are the sheep, Gentiles who have been judged in the "Valley of Jehoshaphat" and invited into the Kingdom of Heaven (Matthew 25:31-46). This also explains how rebellion eventually creeps into the Kingdom.

We read in the book of Zechariah that some nations will refuse to come to Jerusalem during the Feast of Tabernacles. Understand, this will take place while the Messiah Himself will be reigning in Jerusalem (Zechariah 14:16-21).

DISTINCTION AGAIN

The principle of distinction stays during this time, Jew from Gentile, Israel from the nations. Remember, the Messianic Kingdom pulls all things back toward God's original design and intention. The Kingdom to come is a restorative age. Afterward the theme becomes everything new: New Heaven, New Earth, no more oceans!

In the restorative period, the Messianic Kingdom, man will finally grasp his rightful place in this universe, and all the earth will witness Israel's calling and purpose of Jewish survival. Capture some of the glorious transformations that will occur in the Kingdom to come:

During this time, all competition between human and human will be gone. Competition in the church will be gone. Those long turned off to religion will at last find religious solidarity, as one faith, one Messiah, and one religious system will exist, and every nation and tongue will worship the Lord God of Abraham, Isaac, and Jacob.

Also, mourning will give way to joy as death will give way to life, and war will give way to peace. Human government will finally yield to the righteous rule of the Messianic Kingdom, and Jerusalem will be its capital city. Nature will be wonderfully transformed, as the lion will eat straw like the ox, and lay next to the lamb. Mothers will no longer experience miscarriage or children die prematurely, and sickness and disease along with infant mortality will be of the past.

Finally, political genocide and ethnic cleansing will be of a past age because the Messianic Kingdom will bring a completely universal and righteous government. Something that has never occurred, peace will finally be at Israel's borders as God will return the Jewish people to their full and restored homeland, the Promised Land.[1] I believe God will also return the nations back to their God-given geographic boundaries.

PURPOSE OF THE FUTURE KINGDOM

Now to the purpose of the future Messianic Kingdom. Daniel pinpoints this Kingdom far into the future of himself when he writes: *"...The wind swept them away without leaving a trace. But the rock that struck the statue became a huge mountain and filled the whole earth"* (Daniel 2:35 NIV).

God will usher in the most ideal time since the Garden of Eden era. The age-old teaching of replacement theology will be no more. The thousands of ecclesiastical orders and religious denominations will cease.

Finally, the words of Isaiah and the Psalms become reality: *"...For out of Zion shall go forth the law and the word of the Lord from Jerusalem"* (Isaiah 2:3 NKJV).

The Psalms focus upon this future time: *"If I forget thee, O Jerusalem, let my right hand forget her cunning. If I do not remember thee, let my tongue cleave to the roof of my mouth; if I prefer not Jerusalem above my chief joy"* (Psalm 137:5-6 KJV).

ALL CREATION GROANS

Throughout Jewish history, the Messianic Kingdom has been longed for and prayed for. Always they envisioned Israel restored to her former glory and living in their fullness under the leadership of their Messiah; this is true today as well. The Christian church has also longed for it.

The Christian focus is often upon such images and realities as the cross, the resurrection, the ascension, and Heaven. The Jew sees Jerusalem and Mount Zion restored, while the Christian again sees the "New Jerusalem" coming down out of Heaven as seen in Revelation 21:2. The Kingdom of God has permeated Christian teaching, while the Kingdom of Heaven has permeated Judaism.

7

THE KINGDOM OF GOD VERSUS THE KINGDOM OF HEAVEN

WHEN CONSIDERING THE KINGDOM FURTHER, LET US TOUCH again upon the principle of distinction. Certainly, the Kingdom of Heaven is inseparable from the Kingdom of God. In fact, no dimension of life is outside of it. The very cosmos and beyond is in the Kingdom of God. This is because the Kingdom of God is unlimited, sovereign, timeless, and is over all creation.

The psalmist in chapter 39 expresses a similar sentiment, *"Such knowledge is too wonderful for me, too lofty for me to attain. Where can I go from your Spirit? Where can I flee from your presence? If I go up to the heavens, you are there; if I make my bed in the depths, you are there"* (Psalm 139:6-8 NIV).

Yet, the Kingdom of Heaven is not limitless. It lasts for 1,000 years, and its sovereignty is over the earth. It is material, earthly, and at the same time spiritual. Only after the 1,000 years does the Kingdom of Heaven become the Kingdom God within each other. This is seen in Revelation:

> *The seventh angel sounded his trumpet, and there were loud voices in heaven, which said: "The kingdom of the world has become the kingdom of our Lord and of his Messiah, and he will reign for ever and ever"* (Revelation 11:15 NIV).

One additional passage:

> *Then I saw "a new heaven and a new earth," for the first heaven and the first earth had passed away, and there was no longer any sea. I saw the Holy City, the new Jerusalem, coming down out of heaven from God, prepared as a bride beautifully dressed for her husband* (Revelation 21:1-2 NIV).

KINGDOM GOVERNMENT AND ORDER

In order to gain deeper insight into our future, the Scriptures reveal that the faithful individuals of the past will maintain their purpose even after their passing. There will be a resurrection at the end times, bringing them into the Messianic Kingdom (Daniel 12:2; Revelation 20:12-13; Acts 17:31; Acts 24:15; Matthew 25:31-32; 1 Corinthians 15:12).

All the individuals mentioned in Hebrews 11, and even more, will be restored. Jews and Gentiles will serve together while maintaining their unique identities and fulfilling distinct roles. Humanity will finally progress toward the destinies assigned to them by God.

Emphasizing the principle of distinction between Jews and Gentiles is crucial here, while also recognizing that all individuals are equal. Israel will maintain its special status among nations, and the Jewish people will retain their distinctiveness from the Gentiles.

A profound transformation will occur when all individuals are redeemed and living up to their fullest potential, illuminated by the light of the Messiah. In such a state, feelings of jealousy, self-promotion, and human ambition will cease to exist.

Various aspects, including the principle of governance, highlight this distinction. The concept of government offers insight into Israel's chosen status and their fulfillment of purpose as the chosen people.

We can consider the significance of government in Peter's actions of replacing Judas, one of the twelve apostles, as described in Acts 1:25-26. It was necessary to have twelve apostles to complete a governmental structure. These twelve apostles were appointed to rule over the twelve tribes of Israel after Israel's national restoration.

Another example is the ascension gifts that Yeshua gave before He ascended: *apostle, prophet, evangelist, pastor,* and *teacher.* These offices formed a governmental structure to maintain order (Ephesians 4:9-14).

COMPLETING GOD'S ORDER

To complete this future order, we introduce back to the earth the former King David who will return to reign under King Yeshua as prince over earthly Israel. David can't be the

Crowned Head of course, because Yeshua will be on the throne as the ultimate monarch King.

David will be just one of many princely rulers. One can see this in the following: *"Afterward the Israelites will return and seek the Lord their God and David their king. They will come trembling to the Lord and to his blessings in the last days"* (Hosea 3:5 NIV).

The prophet Jeremiah also reveals that the Jewish people will finally seek the One True God when at the same time, they have David, their king: *"But they shall serve the Lord their God, and David their king, whom I will raise up unto them"* (Jeremiah 30:9 KJV). Other Jewish prophets envisioned a time when David would return:

> *I will place over them one shepherd, my servant David, and he will tend them; he will tend them and be their shepherd. I the Lord will be their God and my servant David will be prince among them. I the Lord have spoken* (Ezekiel 34:23-24 NIV).

THE TWELVE JEWISH APOSTLES

Matthew and Luke provide information regarding the twelve apostles who will literally rule over the nation of Israel after Israel's national regeneration. Jesus said to them, *"Assuredly I say to you, that in the regeneration, when the Son of Man sits on the throne of His glory, you who have followed Me will also sit on twelve thrones, judging the twelve tribes of Israel"* (Matthew 19:28 NKJV).

Also, *"You are those who have stood by me in my trials. And I confer on you a kingdom, just as my Father conferred one on me, so that you may eat and drink at my table in my kingdom and sit on thrones, judging the twelve tribes of Israel"* (Luke 22:28-30 NIV).

ABRAHAM, ISAAC, AND JACOB RETURN

Matthew 8:11 (KJV) states, *"And I say unto you, That many shall come from the east and west, and shall sit down with Abraham, and Isaac, and Jacob, in the kingdom of heaven."* Abraham, Isaac, and Jacob will also be resurrected in the Messianic Kingdom, and many will come from the east and the west to sit down with them.

RIGHTEOUS JUDGES AND COUNSELORS

What has never taken place before, the slighted scales of justice will no longer serve the wealthy and influential alone: *"Behold, a king shall reign in righteousness, and princes shall rule in judgment"* (Isaiah 32:1 KJV). From Ezekiel, *"In the land shall be his possession in Israel: and my princes shall no more oppress my people; and the rest of the land shall they give to the house of Israel according to their tribes"* (Ezekiel 45:8 KJV).

Isaiah carries this same theme regarding judges and counselors: *"I will restore your judges as at the first, and your counselors as at the beginning. Afterward you shall be called the city of righteousness, the faithful city"* (Isaiah 1:26 NKJV).

MORE ON THE END-TIME RESURRECTION

As noted earlier, all will return by way of an end-time resurrection. Often these are associated with great advances in the Kingdom. The tombs broke open and the bodies of many holy people were raised to life (Matthew 27:52).

In the future, the biblical forefathers will return via the same way, giving every nation an opportunity to sit down with them in Jerusalem. *"And I say unto you, That many shall come from the east and west, and shall sit down with Abraham, and Isaac, and Jacob, in the kingdom of heaven"* (Matthew 8:11 KJV).

Finally, Daniel speaks of this fascinating future event in chapter 11 in the last three verses. He deals with the redemption of Israel: *"And many of those who sleep in the dust of the earth shall awake, some to everlasting life, some to shame and everlasting contempt"* (Daniel 12:2 NKJV). Daniel does not say all of them, but many of them that sleep (the righteous who have fallen asleep in the former age) will return to usher in a Davidic order upon the earth.

Specifically, after the final three and a half years of the tribulation, Daniel is told to wait an additional forty-five days. This totals 1,335 days from the abomination in the temple. Daniel is assured here that he and all the Old Testament saints have a vital part in the Kingdom to come:

> *Go thy way, Daniel: for the words are closed up and sealed till the time of the end. Many shall be purified, and made white, and tried; but the wicked shall do wickedly: and none of*

the wicked shall understand, but the wise shall understand. And from the time that the daily sacrifice shall be taken away, and the abomination that maketh desolate set up, there shall be a thousand two hundred and ninety days. Blessed is he that waiteth, and cometh to the thousand three hundred and five and thirty days. But go thou thy way till the end be: for thou shalt rest, and stand in thy lot at the end of the days (Daniel 12:9-13 KJV).

CONCLUSION

The Kingdom that all creation has been groaning for, is a global dream for every nation and tongue (Romans 8:22). Personally, I groan inwardly for God's order to come more and more today. In it, the Jewish people will finally arise and call Him blessed.

Like a crowd cheering on their runner who is about to cross the finish line, we await all Israel coming to faith. This will not be some private event. The whole world will share in the glory of the great finale, which the enemy has sought to destroy through the ages. Oh, beloved, how good and pleasant it will be for both Jew and Gentile—*hineh ma Tov u-mah na'im achim.*

Last, some Gentiles might feel excluded due to so much attention on Israel and the Jewish people. Consider these words of Isaiah, who provides a beautiful portrayal of the future temple ministry that awaits both Jew and Gentile:

Also the sons of the foreigner who join themselves to the Lord, to serve Him, and to love the name of the Lord, to be His servants—everyone who keeps from defiling the Sabbath, and holds fast My covenant—even them I will bring to My holy mountain, and make them joyful in My house of prayer. Their burnt offerings and their sacrifices will be accepted on My altar; for My house shall be called a house of prayer for all nations." The Lord God, who gathers the outcasts of Israel, says, "Yet I will gather to him others besides those who are gathered to him" (Isaiah 56:6-8 NKJV).

8

THE BIBLICAL FEASTS: KINGDOM TIMES AND RHYTHMS

NOTHING CAPTURES THE RESTORATION OF THE JEWISH root today and the Kingdom to come, as the resurgence of the biblical feasts, the festivals of the Lord. Yeshua Jesus observed them all![1] One could characterize the feasts as antidotal and prescriptive, and an introduction to such realities as sanctified time, rhythms of life, and God's concept of time.

The feasts come not from the body of rabbinic literature or tradition, but from the enduring Torah, the first five books of the Old Testament. According to Timothy, this portion of the Bible is a vital part of the entire Word of God: *"All Scripture is God-breathed..."* (2 Timothy 3:16 NIV). Paul first wrote these words to Timothy when only the Torah was in view.

The feasts are commanded by God to be observed perpetually, *"And ye shall keep it a feast unto the Lord seven days in the year. It shall be a statute forever in your generations"* (Leviticus 23:41 KJV). This brings us to the Hebrew word for "forever," which is *olam,* which also describes God's name (Exodus 3:14-15).

In Leviticus 23:1-2 (NKJV), the same idea is found: *"Speak to the children of Israel, and say to them: 'The feasts of the Lord, which you shall proclaim to be holy convocations, these are My feasts.'"*

The writings of Heschel on the Jewish calendar are foundational. Abraham Heschel was a Polish-born Rabbi who lived from 1907-1972. He writes of the feasts and Sabbath in his book, *The Sabbath: Its Meaning for Modern Man*: "The Bible is more concerned with time than space, emphasizing generations and events more than things or lands. It speaks the language of history rather than geography." Feasts like the Sabbath became a holy space in life, and a time to recall history and identity.

Heschel asserts, "Judaism can be characterized as a religion aiming at the sanctification of time...there are no two hours alike. Every hour is unique and the only one given at the moment." More, "Jewish ritual is God's architecture of time—observances are predicted on the phases and rhythms of time."[2]

A rabbinic explanation illustrates the richness of the feasts this way, "The feasts stand on two legs, one in heaven, and one on this earth, and it is impossible to divide them. Take God out of any festival or memorial and you take away one of its legs and it falls flat." Being far more than celebrations, each feast was an *inner spiritual activity* for the Jew. So

Judaism is always reinforcing the Jewish concept that He is the Creative Guiding Force or the Source of All That Is.

The Human Need for Memorials

When God ordered the Israelites to observe the biblical feasts, regularly, according to appointed times, they were to mark a holy time, purpose, and message. It was also a time for God to be worshipped and remembered. When God directed Moses to give to Pharaoh the plain reason he should let His people go, He said: "Let my people go that they may worship Me." Pharaoh prevented the Israelites from remembering God at His appointed time.

Samson Raphael Hirsch (1808-1888) said a hundred years ago, "The Jew's catechism is his calendar," when he called upon his contemporaries to count and live their days accorded to the hallowed order and rhythm of the Jewish calendar (which is of course the biblical calendar.)"

Any notion then of *hallowed order* and *rhythms* or *numbering of our days* and *architecture of time,* one is confronted immediately with an obvious nugget in the treasure of God; *the feasts were given as memorials to be observed forever, from the age past and into the present age, and into the age to come.* Even in the Kingdom to come, all humankind, Jew and Gentile, will be required to observe the Feast of Tabernacles. Recall that during this time, Yeshua Himself will be reigning upon His throne in Jerusalem (Zechariah 14:16).

What becomes evident is the human inclination to forget God and His principles. Out of Israel's forty-two kings who reigned, only nine did right in the eyes of the Lord, yes only nine. The Psalmist in chapter 78:32 (NIV) answers this mystery: *"In spite of all this they kept on sinning; in spite of his wonders, they did not believe."* Man's tenacious bout with the same touches all. Man loses his way and must always be brought back to remembrance. An ancient Jewish sage sums it up this way, "As water and fire cannot coexist in the same vessel, so too, love of this world and love of the World to Come are like two wives of the same husband: please one, the other gets angry." How much more for us in Messiah's glorious truth!

THE CALENDAR

Regarding the calendar, biblical rhythms need to be calibrated according to our modern civil calendar that Pope Gregory instituted in 1582. His calendar defiled the biblical calendar to its core.

The Gregorian calendar was purely solar, while the ancient Israelites calendar was luni-solar and followed closely the course of the moon to the next moon. Yet the lunar months corresponded to the season of the year, which is governed by the sun. Immediately one sees the close relationship to harvest and planting.

Our modern-day calendar year consists of 365 days. There are fewer than 100 Sabbaths, feast days, fast days, and holidays, and there are more ordinary days than special days.

Roman Days and Months

To grasp how completely the biblical calendar was defiled, consider our modern days and months. The month of January or Januarious was named for Janus, the god of doors. February or Briareus comes from the festival of forgiveness of sins. March or Martius was derived from Mars, the Roman god of war. April or Aprils is derived from the dedication to the goddess Venus. May or Maius is derived from the goddess Maia. June or Junius is named after the goddess Juna. July and August were named after Julius Caesar and Augustus. December was originally the tenth month on the Roman calendar.

When it comes to the days of the week, the Greeks derived their names from the sun, moon, and five known planets; these were in turn named after the Greek gods: Ares, Hermes, Zeus, Aphrodite, and Cronus. They called the days of week *theon hemerai* (days of the gods). The Romans substituted their equivalent gods for the Greek gods Mars, Mercury, Jove (Jupiter), Venus, and Saturn.

Contrary to the Romans and Greeks, the Bible designates Shabbat-Sabbath from all other days; six days we labor, but on the seventh is a Sabbath! Our modern days trace back to the following:

- Sunday came from Sun's Day or the day of the sun.

- Monday from Moon's Day.

- Tuesday was derived from *Tiu's* Day for the English Germanic god of war and sky.

- Wednesday from *Woden's* Day, the leader of the Wild Hun.

- Thursday, from *Thor's* Day, named for the god of thunder. He is also represented as riding a chariot drawn by goats and is the defender of the Aesir.

- Friday comes from *Freya* or *Fria,* who is the Teutonic/Germanic people's goddess of love, beauty and procreation.

- Saturday (the biblical Sabbath) came from the planet Saturn who was also known as the god of agriculture and harvest. Saturn's wife Opis was the goddess of fertility, and the Greeks and later mythologists believed they ruled the earth during the time of happiness and virtue, which is ironic since holiness, happiness, and virtue are the qualities that the One True God intended for His people on Shabbat.

What the Spirit of God has initiated today is nothing short of redeeming time and restoring biblical rhythms. This defined not only ancient Israel and the early body of Jewish believers, it characterizes the Kingdom to come.

In Part II we explore how Constantine interfered further and set the course in motion further away from Jewish understanding, and how anti-Semitism permeated his new ecclesiastical system.

PART II

CONSTANTINE'S
INTERFERENCE

CONSTANTINE INTERFERED WITH THE DAYS AND TIMES and Easter. In 380, Roman Emperor Constantine made Christianity an officially recognized religion by the state, bringing relief to countless Christians enduring severe persecution. Emperor Tragan had described Christians as being out of sync with the prevailing spirit of the time.

However, Constantine's introduction of a new ecclesiastical calendar disregarded Jewish customs and pushed forward a different set of practices within the church.

Constantine established the revered day of the Sun (Sunday), which led to the closure of law courts and workshops on that day. Only benevolent activities were permitted. His disapproval of Jewish forms of worship and culture once again reinforced the perception that the Jewish people were excluded from God's chosen ones. From their perspective, Constantine's ecclesiastical system disavowed the Jewish roots of Christianity.

At the Council of Nicaea in the year 323, Constantine and his bishops determined that Easter would never again be celebrated on the Jewish Passover. Following this ruling, the feast of the resurrection was required to be celebrated everywhere on a Sunday and would always be on the fourteenth of *Nisan*, the Sunday after the vernal full moon. If the full moon should occur on a Sunday and coincide with the Passover festival, Easter would be commemorated on the Sunday following.

The following circular of Constantine references the rulings that took place at the Council of Nicea:

We should have nothing in common with the most hostile people, the Jews; for we have received from the Redeemer another way of honoring God (the order of the days of the week,) and harmoniously adopting this method, we would withdraw ourselves from the evil fellowship of the Jews. For what they pompously assert, is really utterly absurd: that we cannot keep this feast at all without their instruction.

According to the Council of Nicaea, the Jewish Feast of First Fruits, also known as the resurrection feast, was substituted with Easter, a spring festival associated with the pagan worship of Ishtar. The following is an excerpt from Constantine's letter and decree at the Council of Nicaea:

And truly, in the first place, it seemed to everyone a most unworthy thing that we should follow the custom of the Jews in the celebration of this most holy solemnity, who, polluted wretches! Having stained their hands with a nefarious crime, are justly blinded in their minds. It is fit therefore, that rejecting the practice of this people we should perpetuate to all ages the celebration of this rite, in a more lawful order, which we have kept from the first day of Lord's passion even to the present times. Let us then have nothing in common with the most hostile rabble of the Jews. We have received another method from the Savior. Wherefore, that a suitable reformation should take place in this respect [substituting Easter in the place of Passover], and that one rule should be followed, is the will of divine providence, as all I think, must perceive. As it is necessary that this fault be amended that we have nothing in common with the usage of these parricides and murderers of our Lord—and to have no fellowship with the perjury of the Jews. These being the case receive with cheerfulness the heavenly and truly divine command. For whatever is transacted in the holy council of bishops, is to be referred to the divine will.[1]

Ironically, the one religion that opposed all the excessive paganism of the day was Judaism. Constantine's Christianity (early Catholicism) was an empire religion, where Jews were forced to exchange Judaism (the belief in a monotheistic God) for a form of paganism, the worship of saints, statues, and a culture of graven images. Roman Christianity enforced uniformity.

Judaism on the other hand, engaged the hearts of all people. Judaism as seen in the central sanctuary in Jerusalem was called a House of Prayer for all nations. Even during Succoth, seventy offerings of bullocks were offered on behalf of the nations.

Judaism taught that the blessing of each was to always rise to the benefit to all: *"If only the nations had realized how much they benefited from the Temple service, they would have dispatched troops to protect it from attack"* (Bamidbar Rabbah 1:3).

CONCLUSION

It is sufficient to say, that the same failures that caused Israel to be scattered among the nations according to the Talmud applies to all of us: "the approaches to the nations that they desired," in this we are not so different (Pesachim188b).

When we are brought into remembrance of God, separation and distinction is achieved again. For this reason, when Yeshua completed His last Passover, He said these words: *"Do this in remembrance of me"* (1 Corinthians 11:24 NIV). Yeshua made clear that we always need our memory restored and our identity renewed. Renewal of identity is a central work in any revival.

Today, both Jew and Gentile are observing the Feasts together. Churches are regularly holding Passover and Tabernacle services and celebrations. When all is done in the freedom of the Spirit and the reality of God's grace, a biblical rhythm and life emerges that is a shadow of the Kingdom to come. It becomes a blessing to all and a witness to the Jewish community.

9

THE JEWISH ROOT SEVERED

How and when the Jewish root was severed from New Covenant faith (Christianity), explores the very bedrock of Christianity itself, seeing that Judaism is the precursor or parent of the Christian faith.

Consider the fact that believing in Yeshua is a belief that is two thousand years old and began not with a group of marginally observant Jews but Orthodox. It wasn't until the year 313 that Constantine issued the Edict of Milan, which made Christianity an official religion. Soon after, Christianity became the official religion of the Roman empire.

From the beginning, Yeshua was seen as a Jewish scholar and prophet; His message was radical to the religious establishment and mystified the greatest scholars of His day. His miracles captured the attention of the multitudes because only the Messiah could carry them out, like delivering the *"demon-possessed man who was blind and mute"* in Matthew 12.

Born of a Jewish mother and raised by her and her husband, Joseph, Yeshua was circumcised on the eighth day and was brought up to fulfill the commandments of the Torah. He likely recited the ancient Psalms, the Eighteen Benedictions, also the *Avino Malkenu* (Our Father Our King). He came from the tribe of Judah of the line of David and from a priestly clan of the highest order that predated even the Aaronic and Levitical priesthood, the line of Melchizedek (Genesis 14:18; Psalm 110:1,4; Zechariah 6:13; Hebrews 5:1,4-10, 6:20, 7:1).

Yet throughout church history and into our present day, Yeshua has been presented to the Jewish people with a prerequisite of forsaking their own Jewish cultural heritage. Imagine Paul, a former Pharisee (Acts 22:3-4), standing in the synagogue in Pisidian, Antioch, giving testimony that God brought Israel the Messiah, the One from the line of David, and having to give up his Jewish identity (Acts 13:23).

Consider Peter, a former Pharisee himself who lived a life according to the strict dietary laws of Judaism only to become the rock upon which the Jewish Messiah would build His church (Acts 11:4-9).

When exploring the Torah, particularly Numbers 15:38-41 and Deuteronomy 22:12, we see that Yeshua and all Orthodox Jewish males were required to wear fringes on their garments called *tzizit*, which represented the commandments. In Matthew 9:21, we read of a woman who presses through the crowd in order to touch these fringes. On this day however, she was touching the living commandments because the Word had become flesh.

Then consider Revelation 22:18-19 with its strong warning against altering the Word of God, similar to the teaching in the Jewish Talmud in Sanhedrin 90: "If one prophesies as to eradicate a law from the Torah, he is liable to death." Finally, when it comes Yeshua's end-time warnings that are given in 2 Timothy 3:19 and Matthew 10:35, the Talmud has similar warnings:

> In the footsteps of the Messiah insolence will increase, youths will put old men to shame, the old will stand up in the presence of the young, a son will revile his father, a daughter will rise against her mother, a daughter-in-law against her mother-in-law and a man's enemies will be the members of his household. The face of the generation will be like the face of a dog (impervious to shame). A son will not feel ashamed before his father, so upon whom is it for us to rely upon? Upon our Father who is in heaven; man will become more and more debased (Sotah 49b).

A religious leader approached Yeshua one day and asked Him what the greatest commandment in the Law was. He said, *"'Love the Lord your God with all your heart and with all your soul and with all your mind.' This is the first and greatest commandment. And the second is like it: 'Love your neighbor as yourself.' All the Law and the Prophets hang on these two commandments"* (Matthew 22:37-40 NIV).

When asked to sum up Judaism in few moments, Hillel, the great Palestinian sage, echoed the same, "That which is hurtful to thee, do not do to thy neighbor, this is the whole doctrine, the rest is commentary, now go forth and learn."

The Jewish understanding of "neighbor" in most contexts and including Matthew refers to fellow Israelites, countrymen. This important meaning is often missed. In Exodus 20:16, it speaks about bearing false witness against thy neighbor, which meant your fellow Israelite, brother, companion, husband, even lover. It refers to those with whom you are in relationship and are equally yoked. For us today, it refers to believers.

In other words, Scripture provides specific instructions on how brothers and sisters in the Lord are to treat one another. Ephesians 4:25 (NIV) says, *"Therefore each of you must put off falsehood and speak truthfully to your neighbor, for we are all members of one body."*

An important truth is that we cannot love another if we do not love ourself first. By extension, the body of Messiah cannot truly love the world if it has not learned to love one another.

EMPIRE LIFE BECOMES DIFFICULT ON JEWS

The establishment of a separate Gentile Christian expression, distinct from Judaism, was of utmost importance for the new institutional church. A new foundation needed to be established, deviating from the original Jewish foundation.

The circumstances of life within the Roman Empire made it challenging for early Jewish followers of Jesus, particularly because they adhered to circumcision and a system of festal observances alien to the Roman Empire. Great pressure was exerted on them to abandon the bedrock practices of Judaism.

Regarding the new Christian church, they recognized the authority of the Empire and incorporated certain Roman religious customs and traditions into their practices.

These included adopting Sunday as the day of worship instead of the Sabbath as given in the Torah, incorporating Easter and other holidays from the pagan Roman calendar, and utilizing symbols and artwork previously associated with pagan temples. Essentially, Gentile Christian churches were established on a Roman foundation. This facilitated the spread of Christianity throughout the Roman Empire, starting from Jerusalem, reaching Rome, and eventually extending to the entire world.

ANTI-JEWISH PATTERNS

Earlier, we recognized and discussed the devastation caused by the destruction of the temple and how early leaders in the church attributed God's supposed rejection of His people to the Jewish community, holding them responsible for the death of Yeshua. We also examined the consequences of Constantine's anti-Jewish decrees and judgments, which led to a long-standing atmosphere of hostility toward Jews and the historical persecutions mentioned earlier in this book.

Essentially, the divergence between Christianity and Judaism occurred gradually over time, rather than from one catastrophic incident. But from these events, and the patterns of thinking that followed, the early church fostered anti-Jewish paradigms, theologies, and heart attitudes creating biased views against Jews for generations. This was perpetuated from seminary to seminary and denomination to denomination.

Even in our modern day, one can see how such terms as *Christ, church, crusade, conversion,* and *cross* form their own "crown of thorns" for Jewish people, as Christianity was branded as a religion that brought much anti-Semitism and suffering.

JEWS AND THE ROMAN WORLD

If one were to research Christian church history, particularly in the time of Paul, one would discover a growing hostility between the Jewish and early new Roman worlds. This is brought to light in the words of Cicero, who was a politician and philosopher before the destruction of the second temple:

> Even while Jerusalem was still standing, the Jews were at peace with us. The practice of their sacred rites, however, were at variance with the glory of our empire, the dignity of our name, and the customs of our ancestors.[1]

As Cicero notes, the Roman Christian world was an empire religion that was in direct opposition to the Messianic-type rule that Jews longed for. Jews wanting to embrace Yeshua, and many did for cultural, political, and economic reasons, had to renounce their Jewish identity and turn from the faith of their biblical ancestors; Jews were forced to convert to a Gentile form of faith.

In his book *Restoring the Jewishness of the Gospel*, David Stern notes that the Jews were required to swear to and sign the following:

> I renounce all customs, rites, legalisms, unleavened breads and sacrifices of lambs of the Hebrews, and all the other Feasts of the Hebrews, sacrifices, prayers, aspersions, purifications, sanctifications, and propitiations, and fasts, and new moons, and Sabbaths, and superstitions, and hymns and chants and observances and synagogues, and the food and drink of the Hebrews. In a word, I renounce absolutely everything Jewish, every law, rite and custom—and if afterward I shall wish to deny and return to Jewish superstitions, or shall be found eating with Jews, or feasting with them, or secretly conversing and condemning the Christian religion instead of openly confuting them and condemning their vain faith, then let the trembling of Cain and the leprosy of Gehazi cleave to me, as well as the legal punishments to which I acknowledge myself liable. And may I be an anathema in the world to come, and my soul be set down with Satan and the devils.[2]

THE BLINDNESS OF EARLY CHURCH FATHERS

Following then in the early mindset toward Jews and Judaism, early church fathers began inculcating the early church with anti-Jewish thinking and attitudes. If this message appears again and again, it is because anti-Jewish thinking was like a torrent of anti-Semitism running through the center of the early Judeo-Christian and Roman world. It cut a divide through the heart of Judaism that separated the Jew from the Gentile for centuries forward.

Consider the following men who greatly influenced the church, often out of the Catholic world. Catholicism was the crucible of early Christian thought. Reflect on such men as Saint Gregory of Nyssa (335–394), Saint Augustine (354–430), Saint Jerome (374–419), Pope Innocent III (1160/61–1216), and Pope Pious IV (1499–1565).

The following are some words of *Pope Pious* and excerpts from other early church leaders:

> Until today, in truth, the Jews are scandalized when they hear that God was scourged, was crucified, and that He died, holding it unworthy so much as to hear that God endured things unworthily.... The Jews who deny that Messiah has come and that He is God, lies. Herod is the devil, the Jews demons; that one is King of the Jews, this one the King of demons. (Pope Pious IV)

Martin Luther

The second individual came out of the reformation of the 1500s, Martin Luther (1483–1546). Though he delivered correction to the dark Catholic world at the time and spawned the Reformation, his spirit became embittered toward the Jews when they continually pushed away his efforts to convert them early in his ministry.

Luther began to pour out venomous rebukes of them, his sermons were an exhibition of pure Jewish hate that framed Christianity as harsh, unforgiving, and anti-Semitic. His sermons are well-known in Judaism today. The following are excerpts from Martin Luther's *The Jew and Their Lies* (1543).[3]

> What then shall we Christians do with this damned, rejected race of Jews? Since they live among us and we know about they're lying, blasphemy, and cursing, we cannot tolerate them if we do not wish to share in their lies, curses, and blasphemy.
>
> In this way, we cannot quench the inextinguishable fire of divine rage (as the prophets say) nor convert the Jews. We must prayerfully and reverentially practice a merciful severity. Perhaps we may save a few from the fire and the flames. We must not seek vengeance. They are surely being punished a thousand times more than we might wish them. Let me give you my honest advice.
>
> First, their synagogues or churches should be set on fire, and whatever does not burn up should be covered or spread over with dirt so that no one may ever be able to see a cinder or stone of it. This ought to be done for the honor of God and of Christianity in order that God may see that we are Christians, and that we have not wittingly tolerated or approved of such public lying, cursing, and blaspheming of His Son and His Christians.

Second, their houses should likewise be broken down and destroyed. For they perpetrate the same things there that they do in their synagogues. For this reason they ought to be put under one roof or in a stable, like gypsies, in order that they may realize that they are not masters in our land, as they boast, but miserable captives, as they complain of us incessantly before God with their bitter wailing.

Third, they should be deprived of their prayer books and Talmud's in which such idolatry, lies, cursing, and blasphemy are taught.

Fourth, their rabbis must be forbidden under threat of death to teach anymore.

Fifth, passport and traveling privileges should be absolutely forbidden to Jews. For they have no business in the rural districts since they are not nobles, nor officials, nor merchants, nor the like. Let them stay at home.

Sixth, they ought to be stopped from usury. All their cash and valuables of silver and gold ought to be taken from them and put aside for safekeeping. For this reason, as said before, everything that they possess they stole and robbed from us through their usury, for they have no other means of support. This money should be used in the case (and in no other) where a Jew has honestly become a Christian, so that he may get for the time being one or two or three hundred florins, as the person may require. This in order, that he may start a business to support his poor wife and children and the old and feeble. Such evilly acquired money is cursed, unless, with God's blessing, it is put to some good and necessary use.

Martin Luther and the Encyclopedia Judaica

The Encyclopedia Judaica writes of Martin Luther: "Short of the Auschwitz oven and extermination, the whole Nazi Holocaust is pre-outlined here."[4] Is it any wonder that Hitler and Julius Streicher quoted Martin Luther as justification for their destruction of 6 million Jews?

John Chrysostom

John Chrysostom is one noteworthy individual, but for the wrong reasons. A bishop of the church at Antioch and considered the greatest preacher of his day, he spoke violently against the Jews. He said there could never be forgiveness for the Jews; God had always hated them. He taught it was the Christian duty to hate the Jews, the Jews were assassins of Christ, worshippers of the devil, that their synagogue was worse than a brothel, a den of scoundrels, a temple of demons devoted to idolatrous cults.[5]

HOW THE CROSS BECAME A SWORD

Justin Martyr (100–165) claimed that God's covenant with the Jews was no longer valid and that Gentiles had replaced Jews in God's redemptive plan.

Ignatius, the bishop of the church in Antioch early in the second century, wrote that anyone who celebrated the Passover with the Jews or received emblems of the Jewish feast was a partaker with those who killed the Lord and His apostles.

Clement of Alexandria (150–215) emphasized Greek philosophy rather than the Tanakh as the primary means God gave the Gentiles to lead them to Jesus as the ultimate Word of God.

Tertullian (160–220) was one of the most important Christian writers of the second century. His works were highly significant in developing the basic doctrines of the church. In one of his writings titled *Against the Jews,* he blamed the entire Jewish race for the death of Jesus.

Eusebius (263–339) wrote the history of the church for the first three centuries. He taught that the promises and blessings of the Tanakh were for the Christians and that the curses were for the Jews. He declared that the church was the "true Israel of God" that had replaced literal Israel in God's covenants.

Jerome (345–420), a great Bible scholar, his Latin translation of the Scriptures became the official Bible of the church. Jerome claimed that the Jews were incapable of understanding the Scriptures and that they should be severely persecuted until they confessed the "true faith."

CONCLUSION

In these recent chapters, we have exposed some of the grave errors of early church leaders. Our lingering focus should be elsewhere. We must gain a historical awareness of Christian church history and its effect on Jewish history. Then and only then can we gain a better understanding of the heart and mind of the Jewish people. Dr. Michael Brown sums it up best in his book, *Our Hands Are Stained with Blood:*

> The Church has indeed sinned terribly against the Jewish people, but not all the Church has sinned. Wherever Jesus has been lifted up and adored, there have always been genuine lovers of Israel. There has been a bloody river of hatred that has flowed through the history of the Church. But there has also been a stream of sacrificial love. It must overflow its banks in our day. Mercy and compassion must arise for the Lord's brothers and sisters in the flesh. One could easily review the Crusades, the Spanish Inquisition, and the Russian Pogroms. Yes, the walls of Church history are open for inspection, but the daunting task of scaling walls of long-held misunderstanding is wonderfully accelerated.[6]

10

THEOLOGICAL THEFTS AND FURTHER SEPARATION

AT THIS POINT, ONE CAN EASILY SEE THAT JEWISH SENTIment in the early Christian church can be placed in two categories: things that separated Christians and Jews, called "discontinuity," and things that united Christians and Jews, simply "continuity."

For the purposes of *discontinuity*, we focus here upon a sequence of theological pilferages—the robbing of biblical truths and precepts that reinforced a historical divide between the Jew and the Gentile.

Doctrines such as salvation, grace, sanctification, and the many glories of New Covenant life are what unite Christians and Jews, which form *continuity*. But through the enemy's involvement in Christian history, we expose the enemy's efforts to rob the church of Jewish election and break *continuity*. Here are some of those thefts.

First Theft: Jewish Interpretation

This first theft that came at a great loss to the Scripture is the allegorical interpretation of Scripture. An allegory is a work in which the characters and events represent other things; they symbolically express a deeper, often spiritual, moral, or political, meaning.

Influential individuals like Origen (185–254) interpreted end-time prophecies through this allegorizing method. But he obliterated the distinction between Israel and the church, Israel and the covenant land, and the relationship between the church and the Jewish people.[1]

Origen's form of interpretation took the reader beyond the Scripture's literal meaning and context so that no one can prove his interpretation. And this is the fundamental problem with allegorizing: Whose interpretation is correct? It often relies upon the most notable and outstanding author or intellectual at the time, like an Origen or an Eusebius type who authored so many volumes of works within the early church.

Origen's ideas influenced the church to regard the Hebrew Scriptures merely as a foreshadow of the New Testament; Israel as a people who have lost their covenantal inheritance and relationship to God. This may be difficult to hear, but as a germ needing a host, institutional Christianity became that host for this form of interpretation. It influenced theologians throughout the centuries and into our present day.

Even pastors in our present day, often demonstrate a certain awkwardness and uncertainty in viewing a particular text plainly when it comes to Israel and the Jewish people.

This can often be attributed to a historical root presence of allegorizing. I can personally attest to it since I was once oriented in it.

In Jewish and Hebraic interpretations of Scripture, a verse must stay within its plain meaning. It sees the prophetic writings and accepts them on their literal basis. The reader is always moving from one reality to the next, amongst symbols and concrete things such as people, and not abstractions as the early and allegorical views taught.

Ironically, certain places in Judaism were also affected by allegorizing. A distinction and conflict developed in the early Palestinian and Alexandrian schools of thought. Those from the Alexandrian schools followed the allegorical method of exegesis even though it was at great odds with the rulings of the Jewish law.[2]

The Talmud records in Aboth 9a that an Alexandrian school degenerated so much from it, the literal sense of the Commandments was rejected for the symbolic. Even the covenant of circumcision, and sacrifices, and holy days were ignored.

To further our point and convey the seriousness of this form of interpretation, the following excerpts and remarks by notable men reveal the acute harm that was done to the Scriptures:

Phillip Schaff: Truly, allegorizing was nothing short of a demonic pal that intruded upon the New Covenant body, and it succeeded! Philip Schaff, the nineteenth-century church historian, notes of Origen:

Even heathens and heretics admired or feared his brilliant talent and vast learning. His knowledge embraced all departments of his day's philology, philosophy, and theology. Origen desires to harmonize the New Testament with the philosophy of Plato, his leaning toward idealism, and His constant desire to find a hidden mystic meaning. Though his allegorical interpretation is ingenious, it often runs away from the text and degenerates into the merest caprice.[3]

Coach Bill McCarthy of the Road to Jerusalem ministry found in recent surveys that more than 60 percent of churches in the United States hold to such views that allegorizing created, like replacement theology (the New Testament church is Israel, the Gentile Christian is the Jew).

Hal Lindsey: According to Hal Lindsey in his book, *The Road to Holocaust:* "The man most responsible for changing the way the Church interpreted prophecy was Origen. A leading teacher of theology and philosophy at the influential catechetical school of Alexandria, Egypt, at the beginning of the third century."

H. Newman: Origen was the first to reduce the allegorical method of interpretation to a system. His method of Scripture interpretation was soon adopted throughout the church, and prevailed throughout the Middle Ages.

Joshua Heschel (1907-1972): Considered to be one of the foremost Jewish theologians of the twentieth century wrote of allegorizing: "The radical use of the method of allegorizing of the Hebrew Bible, the tendency to spiritualize the meaning of its works and to minimize its plain historical sense has made many Christians incapable of understanding or having empathy for what the Holy Land means to the Jewish people and to the authors of the Hebrew Bible, or what the people of Israel means in the flesh, not just as a symbol or as a construct of theologians."

SECOND THEFT: THE WIFE OF JEHOVAH

Another important area victimized by allegorizing was the wife of Jehovah. Yes, in the New Testament, the Bride of Messiah is composed of both Jew and Gentile.

But in the Old Testament, the Wife of Jehovah is composed solely of Israel and is not a foreshadowing of the Bride of Christ. If this critical distinction is not made, an incomplete picture is created concerning the relationship between the Jew and the Gentile, the church, and the Jewish people, and Israel.

This distinction is made in Romans 11:26 (NKJV): *"And so **all Israel** will be saved, as it is written: 'The Deliverer will come out of Zion, and He will turn away ungodliness from Jacob.'"* The *"all Israel"* is not the New Testament Gentile church here. It is the Wife of Jehovah composed of the *"all Israel"*— the Jewish people finally coming back to her Husband.

Though the relationship between Israel, the Wife of Jehovah, and God, has been tumultuous, a wonderful reunion takes place in the future as Romans indicates. Israel is portrayed as a wife who goes through a courtship, marriage, adultery, separation, divorce, punishment, and remarriage, and is finally restored to a life of blessings.

Consider the following passages and the extraordinary language used to describe the relationship between God and Israel:

The Marriage: Ezekiel 16:8 NIV

> Later I passed by, and when I looked at you and saw that were old enough for love, I spread the corner of my garment over you and covered your naked body. I gave you my solemn oath and entered into a covenant with you, declares the Sovereign Lord, and you became mine.

The Great Adultery: Hosea 2:2-4 NIV

> Rebuke your mother, rebuke her, for she is not my wife, and I am not her husband. Let her remove the adulterous look from her face and the unfaithfulness from between her breasts. Otherwise, I will strip her naked and make her as bare as on the day she was born; I will make her like a desert, turn her into a parched land, and slay her with thirst. I will not show my love to her children because they are the children of adultery. (Additional passages: Jeremiah 3:1-5,20; Ezekiel 16:15-34)

The Great Divorce: Jeremiah 3:6-10 NIV

> During the reign of King Josiah, the Lord said to me, "Have you seen what faithless Israel has

done? She has gone up on every high hill and under every spreading tree and has committed adultery there. I thought that after she had done all this she would return to me. But she did not, and her unfaithful sister Judah saw it. I gave faithless Israel her certificate of divorce and sent her away because of all her adulteries. Yet I saw that her unfaithful sister Judah had no fear; she also went out and committed adultery. Because Israel's immorality mattered so little to her, she defiled the land and committed adultery with stone and wood. In spite of all this, her unfaithful sister Judah did not return to me with all her heart, but only in pretense," declares the Lord.

The Great Punishment: Ezekiel 16:35-43 NIV

Therefore, you prostitute, hear the world of the Lord! This is what the Sovereign Lord says: Because you poured out your lust [wealth] and exposed your naked body in your promiscuity with you lovers, and because of all your detestable idols, and because you gave them your children's blood, therefore I am going to gather all your lovers, with whom you found pleasure, those you loved as well as those you hated. I will gather them against you from all around and will strip you in front of them, and they will see you stark naked. I will sentence you to the punishment of women who commit adultery and who shed blood; I will bring on you the blood vengeance of my wrath and jealous anger. Then I will deliver you into the hands of your lovers, and they will tear down your mounds and destroy your lofty shrines. They will strip you of your clothes and take your fine jewelry and leave you stark naked. They will bring a mob against you, who will stone you and hack you to pieces with their swords. They will burn down your houses and inflict punishment on you in the sight of many women. I will put a stop to your prostitution, and you will no longer pay your lovers. Then my wrath against you will subside, and my jealousy will turn away from you; I will be calm and no longer angry. Because you did not remember the days of your youth but enraged me with all these things, I will surely bring down on your head what you have done, declares the Sovereign Lord. Did you not add lewdness to all of your other detestable practices? (See also Hosea 2:6-13).

The Great Remarriage and Restored Blessing: Ezekiel 16:60-63 NIV

Yet I will remember the covenant I made with you in your youth and establish an everlasting covenant with you. Then you will remember your ways and be ashamed when you receive your sisters, both those who are older than you and those who are younger. I will give them to you as daughters, but not on the basis of my covenant with you. So I will establish my covenant with you, and you will know that I am the Lord. Then, when I make atonement for you for all you have done, you will remember and be ashamed and never again open your mouth because of your humiliation, declares the Sovereign Lord. (Also, Isaiah 54:1-8, 62:4-5; Hosea 2:14-23).

THIRD THEFT: WE ARE NOT THE NATIONS

Throughout the biblical period, the term *nations* (a Hebrew idiom) refers not to the Jewish people, but to the Gentiles. Though every people group and nation comprise the *ethnos,* the Greek term for *nations* in our modern thought, the Bible states something different about the Jew.

Continually, the word *gentile* is derived from *goy,* or *goyim* in its plural. It almost always refers to non-Israelites, foreign non-Jews, heathens, or nations. This is seen in Leviticus 20:26 (NIV): *"You are to be holy to me because I, the Lord, am holy, and I have set you apart from the nations to be my own."* Then in the following, Deuteronomy 4:20 (NIV) says: *"But as for you, the Lord took you and brought you out of the iron-smelting furnace, out of Egypt, to be the people of his inheritance, as you now are."*

Luke 21:10-11 (NIV) states: *"Nation* [ethnos] *will rise against nation* [ethnos], *kingdom against kingdom."* It refers to *nation against nation, kingdom against kingdom,* and is a

Hebrew idiom for world wars—not small regional border disputes or skirmishes.

In James 1:1 (NIV): *"...to the twelve tribes scattered among the nations."* Here, the term *nations* is speaking about the Jewish Diaspora at the time (Israelite residents in Gentile countries).

Finally, in Galatians 3:8 (KJV), the word *heathen* brings us back to the word *ethnos*, which indicates foreigners or non-Jews: *"And the scripture, foreseeing that God would justify the heathen through faith, preached before the gospel unto Abraham, saying, In thee shall all nations be blessed."* Many more examples in Scripture can be cited leaving the reader to go deeper.

We are again attempting to restore the natural distinction between the Jew and Gentile, Israel and the nations, as God has persistently shown in Scripture.

FOURTH THEFT: FIRST POSITION

Romans 1:16 (NIV): *"I am not ashamed of the gospel, because it is the power of God that brings salvation to everyone who believes: first to the Jew, then to the Gentile."* The principle of "first," traditionally speaking, has been viewed as a past pattern or a historic startup model to begin the church. One may not put it in exactly these terms, but most Christian thinking is in this context.

The notion that the Jews were first, then; but due to their rejection of their Messiah, the Gentile became first. Later at the close of the age, God will turn His attention to the Jew. This belief, of course, is deeply and historically flawed.

The principle of "first" however, was and is dynamic and forward speaking, and is never static. "First" comes from the Greek word *proton* meaning first in time, place, and in order or importance. Scientifically, a proton carries an inherent positive electric charge. Without it, an atom cannot be formed. This, the Greeks saw, as the fundamental component of the universe.

In like manner, the Jew was the fundamental building component of the body and will again in the end comprise an important element. *"If their rejection* [speaking of the Jews] *is the reconciliation to the world, what will their acceptance be but life from the dead?"* (Romans 11:15).

This passage in Romans 11 depicts the body as deprived of life and needing to be revived. How will this revival come? It will come by way of the Jew. It portrays the return of the Jew as a spiritual defibrillator. A defibrillator actually sends an electric charge across the surface of a heart that has stopped.

CONCLUSION

The "first things first" principle should be compared to such first things first principles as our tithes and all other priorities in our lives. Paul never suggests that the Roman believers should withhold the Gospel from the Gentiles until every Jewish person in the world is reached. Paul uses for the word *first, protos,* that implies a priority, rather than a sequential order of events.

If the Jew was chosen first in *time, place,* and *order, and* the mandate to reach the lost sheep of Israel was conveyed with such clarity and importance by Paul, we should diligently seek ways to comply. What should be earnest in our efforts, resources should come to bear. Together, let us toil for the harvest of Jewish souls.

11

SABBATH AND TORAH

AN IMPORTANT PART OF KINGDOM RESTORATION TODAY, and a foretaste of the Kingdom to come, is the many people observing the Saturday Shabbat (the fourth commandment to rest on the seventh day and honor the Lord). Of course, in any dialogue and debate on this topic, one must choose freely by God's grace and liberty what path they should take. Praise God that our salvation and the means to righteousness are no longer determined by it.

Here, we will touch on some defining moments in the Jewish and Christian world over Sabbath and surface the age-old discussion between Sunday and Saturday Sabbath.

The architect of Roman Christianity was, of course, Emperor Constantine who instituted Sunday as the official day of rest. Certainly, Sunday was beneficial since he was able to retain pagan practices for years, which included the worship of the Roman sun god Mithra. Sunday was the Roman day of worship of this god and comes from the Latin *dies solis* or sun's day. Constantine's edicts and legislations on

Sunday as the new Sabbath in his *Edict of Tolerance* was devastating to the Jews. He was very successful in converting vast numbers of pagans and Jews to Christianity, creating the Roman version of the Christian religion that we know today.

Most agree that following our Lord's ascension, the early believers began gathering on Sunday, the first day of the week, which came to be known as the Lord's Day (Revelation 1). But when the early Jewish believers gathered on Sunday mornings, they did not abstain from Saturday Sabbath. Sunday became an added day of worship and fellowship.

The issue that has been debated throughout Christian church history, is whether Sunday (the Lord's Day) replaced the Saturday Shabbat, which is based on the fourth commandment, *"For in six days the Lord made heaven and earth, the sea, and all that is in them, and rested the seventh day; wherefore the Lord blessed the sabbath day, and hallowed it"* (Exodus 20:11 KJV).

Certainly, in the context of Constantine's sweeping changes, there was a need for another official Sabbath. Judaism was now a rejected religion in the eyes of the early church fathers, and Jews had lost their covenantal inheritance; Saturday worship would have legitimized this defunct and rejected religion and people.

Similarly, the early Jewish believers could not adhere to Sunday observance because it would have legitimized Christianity as a replacement for Judaism. More, it would have violated their very Torah. Clearly, once the Jewish root was severed, these two would never be reconciled.

THE WORDS OF PAUL

The most important voice is the apostle Paul who was an Orthodox Jew. As an observant Jew, Jew of all Jews (1 Corinthians 9:20), Paul would never have abandoned Saturday Sabbath, which would have denied his very Jewish identity. Even Jewish historian Josephus writes, "Violating the Sabbath was one of the greatest hallmarks of covenant disloyalty."[1]

Furthermore, Paul did not find it necessary to replace Saturday with Sunday since, in his perspective, Judaism had reached its fulfillment. This does not imply the emergence of a new entity, such as the Christian church or the commonwealth of the church, intended to supplant the original olive tree representing the spiritual community of Israel. Nor does it entail the substitution of the Saturday Sabbath with a new Sabbath, Sunday. Paul did not see replacement, displacement, or substitution, Paul saw continuity and a continuum of Judaism into its fulfillment.

In Paul's view, the olive tree has fully blossomed, and the Gentiles would be grafted in; Jew and Gentile would be joined together in their allegiance to their Jewish King. Here are his words from Ephesians 2:12 (KJV), *"That at that time ye were without Christ, being aliens from the commonwealth of Israel, and strangers from the covenants of promise, having no hope, and without God in the world."*

PAUL IN THE BOOK OF ACTS

To understand Paul's words on Sabbath, holy days, and law, one must discover him in the book of Acts. One of the best places to understand the context of all his future remarks is found there.

In Acts 24:13-14, Paul addresses rumors suggesting that he violated Jewish laws. He refutes the accusations by saying they could not provide any evidence to support the charges against him. Furthermore, he asserts, he embraces every-thing that aligns with the Law.

Moving on to Acts 25:8 (NIV), Paul proclaims, *"I have done nothing wrong against the Jewish law or against the tem-ple or against Caesar."*

In a powerful conversation with his fellow Jews, Paul passionately explains the Kingdom of God from morning till evening. He endeavors to persuade them about Jesus using references from the Law of Moses and the Prophets.

It is important to note that Paul's arguments would have been untenable if he had been disregarding the core prin-ciple of replacing Saturday with Sunday. Even a contempo-rary of Paul, Philo, expresses the following words regarding the Sabbath: "The sacred seventh day, exceeding sanctity and purity, is a time to regulate one's conduct towards God by the rules of piety and holiness and one's conduct towards men by the rules of humanity and justice."[2]

This refers to The Sabbath Day, not numerous Sabbaths, and holy days. "The" Sabbath is referred to more than forty times in the New International Version of the Bible. Paul often speaks of The Sabbath in the context of the pervasive legalism that existed.

In Paul's day, thirty-nine different kinds of work were forbidden on Sabbath. One can only imagine what Paul was facing when he spoke of it while being surrounded by rabbis who were ingenious legalists:

> No...Grinding, sifting, dyeing, beating, making two cords, weaving two threads, separating two threads, making a knot of two threads, beating smooth with a hammer. And these have further restrictions on their range and meaning.[3]

More of Paul on Sabbath

In Colossians, Paul demonstrates more along this line: *"Therefore do not let anyone judge you by what you eat or drink, or with regard to a religious festival, a New Moon celebration or a Sabbath day. These are a shadow of the things that were to come; the reality, however, is found in Christ"* (Colossians 2:16-17 NIV).

Again, Paul is speaking of Sabbaths, festivals, meats, drinks, and New Moons. Some teach from this same passage that we are no longer under the law of the commandments because we are now in the age of grace, and even Sabbath is no longer required.

When it comes to the law, Paul does state that he died to it in Romans 7:4 so that he may live for God and be joined to the Messiah. But Paul has in view animal sacrifices, the mediation of a high priest, the yoke of the Pharisaical laws, and its regulations that strangled the people.

One can also look at Romans 14:5-6 (NIV) as some do and cite an argument against the Saturday Sabbath keeping:

> *One person considers one day more sacred than another; another considers every day alike. Each of them should be fully convinced in their own mind. Whoever regards one day as special does so to the Lord. Whoever eats meat does so to the Lord, for they give thanks to God; and whoever abstains does so to the Lord and gives thanks to God.*

Those days that are being addressed are specific "fast" days that were instituted by the prophets. Paul, in need of dealing with their immaturity due to their divisions and judgments, seeks to establish essential guidelines for them. The entire context of Romans chapter 14 is clearly dealing with meats, specific foods, and festivals.

SABBATH AND THE GREEKS

When it comes to the Greeks and Romans, Sabbath became a point of contention. In fact, it was often viewed with disdain, and Roman satirists made the Jewish Sabbath a source of one-line-jokes, and a target of ridicule and humor. The famous Stoic philosopher and moralist Seneca wrote about Sabbath: "Jewish superstition, especially the Sabbath, is reprehensible, for by refusing to work every seventh day, they [the Jews] lose a seventh part of their life in idleness, and important matters are neglected."[4]

Greeks and Torah

Perhaps nothing was more consequential on Sabbath, than the Greek translation of the Hebrew Scriptures, the Septuagint. Produced in 250 BCE, the Greek language had no good equivalent word to Torah, *yarah* (the Hebrew meaning for instruction, to hit the mark, or to point the way).

The word the Greeks opted for was *nomos*. This word conveyed a strong legalistic sense that equated to law. *Nomos* is used 190 times in the New Testament and refers to *the law of God, the law of the Spirit of life in Yeshua, the law of sin and death, the law of righteousness, works of law, the end of law, the book of the law, and curse of the law.*[5]

Therefore, Torah came to imply a burdensome and legalistic set of rules and regulations, and gave to generations the notion that one is no longer obligated to obey the Ten Commandments, particularly the fourth commandment to honor the seventh day Sabbath. One could say, Constantine created the coffin for the Jewish root; the Greeks by their interpretation of the word *Torah* nailed it shut.

Ironically, the New Testament Scriptures state that the law is good (1 Timothy 1:8). Again, the law is holy and spiritual (Romans 7:12). Thankfully, our salvation is no longer dependent upon any observance of the law (I am speaking of the Ten Commandments, which includes Sabbath-keeping). But the redemptive life with its accompanying grace and freedom, compels us to obey these commandments given to Moshe (Moses) on Sinai.

Thus, to honor the Sabbath and rest on the seventh day is to honor universal principles and a moral code for humankind on our journey through life. In these, Torah remains relevant for all today.

FINAL WORDS ON SABBATH

Finally, let us consider the Sabbath outside the confines of the Torah (the first five books of the Old Testament) and turn to Isaiah's words as he conveys God's intention for the Sabbath: *"Blessed is the one who does this—the person who holds it fast, who keeps the Sabbath without desecrating it, and keeps their hands from doing any evil"* (Isaiah 56:2 NIV).

> *"If you keep your feet from breaking the Sabbath and from doing as you please on my holy day, if you call the Sabbath a delight and the Lord's holy day honorable, and if you honor it by not going your own way and not doing as you please or speaking idle words, then you will find your joy in the Lord, and I will cause you to ride in triumph on the heights of the land and to feast on the inheritance of your father Jacob." The mouth of the Lord has spoken* (Isaiah 58:13-14 NIV).

> *I will also bless the foreigners who commit themselves to the Lord, who serve him and love his name, who worship him and do not desecrate the Sabbath day of rest, and who hold fast to my covenant. I will bring them to my holy mountain*

of Jerusalem and will fill them with joy in my house of prayer... (Isaiah 56:6-7 NLT).

CONCLUSION

Certainly, great deference should be given to the Ten Commandments, not to righteousness, but in response to a righteous God and His code of living for His children here on earth. Believers, let alone the world, could use such ancient principles today as we discussed.

For the child of God, it is good to recall how we are to love and revere God as this is our call—a calling that brings calm in the tempest of life.

> *Hear, O Israel: The Lord our God, the Lord is one! You shall love the Lord your God with all your heart, with all your soul, and with all your strength. And these words, which I am command you today shall be in your heart* (Deuteronomy 6:4-6 NKJV).

The same passage in Deuteronomy 6:7-9 teaches we must diligently teach our children to love God and to know His ways, to help mold our children's thoughts and actions through teaching His Word, both when arising and going to bed, when walking on the street, and when going about our affairs.

12

MISCONCEPTIONS AND RESTORATIONS: JOHN THE BAPTIST AND ELIJAH

JOHN IS AN IMPOSING FIGURE IN LIGHT OF HIS BRIEF MINistry. Take him out of the Roman citadel, the traditional Christian view, and you discover a devout Jewish servant of God who understood the hour dawning on his nation, Israel, and the hour of Judaism's fulfillment!

For over thirty-five years of knowing my Messiah and hearing the Word taught by numerous teachers, John is seldom the subject of attention. Perhaps it is due to the greater attention of his cousin *Yeshua*. Most likely, it is from the systematic sanitizing of Jewishness from the New Testament. Greek Hellenistic thinking has long obscured John the Baptist, specifically those areas of his relationship to Elijah and his role in Yeshua's earliest days of His ministry.

When John began his public ministry, immediately the multitudes were drawn to him. Israel had sunken into deep spiritual decline and desperation, and the people were earnestly searching for the Messiah, hoping for Israel's regeneration and liberation from Roman rule.

So much so that Josephus, the Jewish historian, records that Herod feared killing John due to his fear of the public. When Herod ordered John to be beheaded, the masses saw the destruction of Herod's army as a judgment from God for doing so.

But no Bible character gained so much attention in such a limited span of time than John. The multitudes from every quarter of the region, including Yeshua Himself, were attracted to him:

> *People went out to him from Jerusalem and all of Judea and the whole region of the Jordan. Confessing their sins, they were baptized by him in the Jordan River. ...Then Jesus came from Galilee to the Jordan to be baptized by John. But John tried to deter him, saying, "I need to be baptized by you, and do you come to me?"* (Matthew 3:5-6,13-14 NIV).

HIS BIRTH AND COMING

Scripture reveals that John the Baptist came out from the desert and the wilderness, growing strong in the spirit until he began his public ministry to Israel (Luke 1). When he springs onto the scene of biblical history, little is known of him, only that a whirlwind of prophetic events had begun:

the long-anticipated Kingdom of Heaven was breaking forth onto the earth.

His father, Zechariah, was from the line of Abia or Abijah, a priestly line (1 Chronicles 24:10); his mother Elizabeth was one of the daughters of Aaron (Luke 1:5). Luke reveals that John's father was filled with the Holy Spirit when he prophesied of their long-awaited Messiah and about his son John (Luke 1:67-69).

John was a devout and zealous Jew, perhaps a former member of the Essenes. He would be considered a strange and unusual fellow today as he was then. He wore clothing made of camel's hair and a leather belt around his waist, and he ate locusts and wild honey (Mark 1:6). Prophets can be rather different from others; they are less inhibited and concerned with what others think; they call out the sins of the people when the average person would be fearful and hesitate. This often makes prophets reliable partners with God.

HISTORICAL MISCONCEPTIONS

Viewing John in the context of our study is to see him in Jewish history standing at its climactic point. Rav Shaul (the apostle Paul) states, *"But when the time had fully come, God sent his Son, born of a woman, born under the law, to redeem those under the law, that we might receive the adoption to sonship"* (Galatians 4:4-5 NIV). His public life began at the end of a period that had experienced four centuries of prophetic stillness, Malachi being the last. He emerges at the end of the Old Covenant period when the New Covenant period was about to begin.

Reclaiming John's Identity

In reclaiming John's Jewish identity, we acknowledge that it has been seriously limited due to Christian misconceptions. This lies first in the belief that he came to start Christianity and baptize Gentiles into Christianity. Upon the least challenged is that he came to start the New Testament church. John was not the innovator of baptism or the herald of Christianity, and he is certainly not a Catholic! So let us begin with what John is most famous for, baptism.

A common misunderstanding is that baptism through immersion was a Christian innovation. In fact, it was a Jewish practice called *mikvah* (Hebrew for *baptism*). Scholars are still determining where John was influenced in his administration, but some believe that John may have been a member of the Essenes. This sect in the Qumran community had pulled back from society to study Torah and await the coming of Messiah. Because they practiced immersion daily, they were called *tovelei shaharit* or "dawn bathers."

Today, the *mikvah* is still administered in the Jewish faith to anyone undergoing ritual baths. These included women following menstruation and childbirth, men seeking to achieve ritual purity, and Gentiles converting to Judaism.

The main idea is that immersion baptism was a widely practiced tradition among Jews, so no one ever questioned John about it. The only disagreement concerning baptism was about the name in which people should be baptized. This can be observed in Paul's letters to the Corinthians, including:

...Were you baptized in the name of Paul? I thank God that I did not baptize any of you except Crispus and Gaius, so no one can say that you were baptized in my name. (Yes, I also baptized the household of Stephanas; beyond that, I don't remember if I baptized anyone else) (1 Corinthians 1:13-16 NIV).

JOHN'S PURPOSE IN COMING

Another source of confusion arose regarding John's purpose for coming. John was tasked with preparing a spiritual and prophetic pathway for the arrival of the Jewish Messiah in Israel. This was the primary focus of John: *"I came baptizing with water"* so Yeshua *"might be revealed to Israel"* (John 1:31 NIV).

This is also illustrated in the account of a Greek woman who came to Yeshua for healing for her daughter. Her daughter had a demon, and the mother knew that Yeshua was the only One who could truly help her daughter. In the following passage, the Gentiles are referred to as dogs, and the children refer to the nation of Israel and the Jews:

Jesus did not answer a word. So his disciples came to him and urged him, "Send her away, for she keeps crying out after us." He answered, "I was sent only to the lost sheep of Israel" (Matthew 15:23-24 NIV).

"First let the children eat all they want," he told her, "for it is not right take the children's bread and toss it to the dogs." "Lord," she replied,

"even the dogs under the table eat the children's crumbs" (Mark 7:27-28 NIV).

John's preaching was always pointing to the coming Messiah and the Kingdom. The Talmud actually describes this time and purpose: "Who will come to usher in the Messianic Age and he will not abrogate justly established laws, but only those arbitrary and lawless decisions" (Tractate Eduyyoth 9b).

The words of Isaiah are also important: *"A voice of one calling: 'In the wilderness prepare the way for the Lord; make straight in the desert a highway for our God'"* (Isaiah 40:3 NIV). The words of prophet Malachi: *"I will send my messenger, who will prepare the way before me..."* (Malachi 3:1 NIV).

Again and again, we see that John came first for the nation of Israel. When the Messiah did come, He rightfully began His work with Israel and His own brethren and tries to relax the priesthood in exchange for new spiritual garments. The prophet Malachi points to this: *"For he will be like a refiner's fire or a launderer's soap. He will sit as a refiner and purifier of silver; he will purify the Levites and refine them like gold and silver..."* (Malachi 3:2-3 NIV).

John and Yeshua had a common mission: get Israel to cross over the New Covenant bridge into a new and fuller form of Judaism. Dr. Daniel Juster calls it a new sect of Judaism seeking to demonstrate that *Yeshua* was indeed the Jewish Messiah—this speaks implicitly to the value and purpose of John's coming.

JOHN AND THE KINGDOM

The topic of the Kingdom has been discussed in detail. But it breaks through everywhere in John's ministry. How John understood it bears much upon the study of John and Israel's political and spiritual life at the time.

John's view of the Kingdom, as all the Jewish believers at that time, was not one that comes at the end of man's natural days, but it was imminent. So, *the kingdom of heaven is near,*" as stated in Matthew 3:2, was understandable.

Questions remain, however, regarding John's life, especially his association with Elijah:

- Was John Elijah?
- Did John fulfill the ministry of Elijah?
- What common elements did John share with Elijah?

These questions are answered in Part III.

PART III

WAS JOHN ELIJAH?

They asked him, "Then who are you? Are you Elijah?" He said, "I am not." "Are you the Prophet?" He answered, "No." Finally they said, "Who are you? Give us an answer to take back to those who sent us. What do you say about yourself?" John replied in the words of Isaiah the prophet, "I am the voice of one calling in the wilderness, 'Make straight the way for the Lord'" (John 1:21-23 NIV).

PLACING THE ABOVE PASSAGE IN THE CONTEXT OF THE previous verse 20 that says, *"He did not fail to confess, but confessed freely, 'I am not the Messiah,'"* it is evident that they were wondering if he was the Christ. John answered three questions correctly and draws their attention to the prophet Isaiah in chapter 40:3, asserting the prophecy in Malachi 3: *"I am a voice of one calling in the desert, 'Prepare the way of the Lord.'"* In another place, we see the same emphasis, but something is added:

Truly I tell you, among those born of women there has not risen anyone greater than John the Baptist; yet whoever is least in the kingdom of heaven is greater than he. From the days of John the Baptist until now, the kingdom of heaven has been subjected to violence, and violent people have been raiding it. For all the Prophets and the Law prophesied until John. And if you are willing to accept it, he is the Elijah who was to come. Whoever has ears, let them hear (Matthew 11:11-15 NIV).

Let me repeat verse 14: *"If you are willing to accept it, he is the Elijah."* Did they accept it? No. Therefore, John did not become their Elijah to national Israel. However, to every Jew who accepted John, they would have accepted Yeshua and automatically received the restorative work of Elijah. In this, John and Elijah share these common elements.

This is brought to light further in a scene when Messiah was speaking to His *talmidim* (disciples) while walking down a mountain with them:

> *And they asked him, "Why do the teachers of the law say that Elijah must come first?" Jesus replied, "To be sure, Elijah does come first, and restores all things. Why then is it written that the Son of Man must suffer much and be rejected? But I tell you, Elijah has come, and they have done to him everything they wished, just as it is written about him"* (Mark 9:11-13 NIV).

Hence, John fulfills Elijah's work for all who were willing to accept him based on Matthew's words in 11:11-15. To conclude, John came to prepare the way for the Messiah's first agenda: to go to the nation of Israel so the righteousness of God's Word would be fulfilled. John came not to plant the first church so Christianity could begin or look for Gentiles to baptize. Although, he baptized all who were willing, so he could testify to the coming and greater One, Yeshua.

In closing, John and Elijah had a common mission and message of restoration and preparation for the Messiah to Israel. Had Israel accepted their Messiah, Israel would have been fully redeemed, the priesthood would have been cleansed, the Hebraic root would have remained, and Elijah's work would have been fully completed. This will all take place in the future, as we all enter the Messianic Kingdom to come.

13

THE GENTILES FIND THEIR CALLING

OF ALL THE MANY UNIQUE FEATURES THAT THE GENTILE relationship with the Jew holds, Israel's redemption is arguably the most important. Isaiah speaks about the salvation and blessing of the Gentiles like no other and emphasizes the importance of the Gentile role in God's plan for the Jew fifteen times. Gentile is stated as often in his writings as it is used in all the rest of the Old Testament. Isaiah's prophecies are the only ones quoted in the Gospels (Matthew 4:15, 12:18; Luke 2:32).

If Paul is considered the apostle to the Gentiles in the New Testament, Isaiah could be the apostle to the Gentiles in the Old Testament. He seems to rejoice in God's plan of salvation for all the nations. In his own words:

This is what the Sovereign Lord says, "See, I will give a signal to the Gentiles, and they shall carry your little sons [Jewish boys] back to you

in their arms, and your daughters [Jewish girls]
on their shoulders (Isaiah 49:22 TLB).

Also, the following:

*And he said, It is a light thing that thou should-
est be my servant to raise up the tribes of Jacob,
and to restore the preserved of Israel: I will also
give thee for a light to the Gentiles, that thou
mayest be my salvation unto the end of the earth*
(Isaiah 49:6 KJV).

As one reviews the extraordinary range of involvement for the Gentile in God's plan for the Jewish people, the Gentile calling is essential to God's plan for the
Jewish people.

One area is the Ruth Calling, a deeply prophetic calling
which is dramatically affecting the Gentiles and bringing
much-needed partnerships to the Messianic Jewish mission.

THE RUTH GENERATION

Many are familiar with the story of Ruth; a woman who
became famous for her compassion for her Jewish mother-
in-law, Naomi. Ruth stated, *"Where you go, I will go, and
where you stay, I will stay. Your people will be my people and
your God my God"* (Ruth 1:16 NIV). The question her statement raises: What does it mean to acknowledge a common
destiny as Ruth did with Naomi?

For one, today it acknowledges oneself in a common
future with the Jew; this is a profound truth with great

relevance. Countless individuals are letting go of their own Gentile church culture to affirm their lot and future with the Jewish people. Often as part of the cost, it can bring separation from loved ones, accusations of converting to Judaism, or even erecting a wall of division; but despite it, they continue.

The real benefit that comes to the body through the Ruth generation is the true understanding of God's heart for His firstborn. They come to be vital partners in the Messianic call, while demonstrating the model of the One New Man that is provoking both to Gentile Christians and the Jewish people. They become end-time light-bearers of God's benevolent nature toward the Jewish people.

ALIYAH, JEWISH RETURN TO THE LAND

When God finally gave to the Jews their homeland in 1948, Jews returning to the land fulfilled what is termed "Aliyah" (Return). The essence of Aliyah is a virulent force in the Jewish people. Many of the Jewish people who return to Israel will do so with the assistance of the Gentiles. And Gentile ministries exist today whose sole purpose is to facilitate the return of the Jewish people.

Thousands are serving as these shepherds' rods pointing the lost sheep of Israel back to Zion.

Jews who live outside Israel, the *Diaspora*, often return to Israel when anti-Semitism begins or economic and political difficulties arise. Some are compelled spiritually and prophetically, and some leave to take part in their own cultural return to live with their people in an entirely Jewish state.

More than 400 Scriptures in the Bible foretell the Jewish people's return to the land of biblical history. The ingathering of the exiles, then, is a timeless principle. Tom Hess's book, *Let My People Go*, is a classic reading for this train of thought. Consider the following:

> *And kings shall be thy nursing fathers and their queens thy nursing mothers: they shall bow down to thee with their face toward the earth, and lick up the dust of thy feet, and thou shalt know that I am the Lord: for they shall not be ashamed that wait for me* (Isaiah 49:23 KJV).

> *Thus saith the Lord of hosts; In those days it shall come to pass, that ten men shall take hold out of all languages of the nations, even shall take hold of the skirt of him that is a Jew, saying, We will go with you: for we have heard that God is with you* (Zechariah 8:23 KJV).

PROVOKING THE JEWS TO ENVY

With the gospel message falling to the Gentiles after Israel rejects her Messiah, the Gentile church has proclaimed the truth of the One True God to virtually every nation and tongue. Yet, the Gentile church was also to provoke the Jewish people to envy, a commission that is given in Romans 11:11 (NIV): the words of Paul, *"Again I ask: Did they stumble so as to fall beyond recovery? Not at all! Rather, because of their transgression, salvation has come to the Gentiles to make Israel envious."*

Moses writes: *"I will make them envious by those who are not a people; I will make them angry by a nation that has no understanding"* (Deuteronomy 32:21 NIV).

Sadly, Christendom has not understood the scriptural understanding of the relationship between the Jew and the Gentile—the Jew and the Christian church.

In this current time, however, God is wonderfully restoring love for the Jewish people and the nation of Israel. He is restoring the Jewish root and making the church a more Jewish-friendly centered place. The body is being prepared to fulfill her final mandate to the Jew.

GENTILES STAND AGAINST ANTI-SEMITISM

Yeshua's return, and the passage at length:

> *When the Son of Man comes in his glory, and all the angels with him, he will sit on his glorious throne. All the nations will be gathered before him, and he will separate the people one from another as a shepherd separates the sheep from the goats. He will put the sheep on his right and the goats on his left. Then the King will say to those on his right, "Come, you who are blessed by my Father; take your inheritance, the kingdom prepared for you since the creation of the world. For I was hungry and you gave me something to eat, I was thirsty and you gave me something to drink, I was a stranger and you invited me in, I needed clothes and you clothed me, I was sick and you looked after me, I was in prison and*

you came to visit me." Then the righteous will answer him, "Lord, when did we see you hungry and feed you, or thirsty and give you something to drink? When did we see you a stranger and invite you in, or needing clothes and clothe you? When did we see you sick or in prison and go to visit you?" The King will reply, "Truly I tell you, whatever you did for one of the least of these brothers and sisters of mine, you did for me." Then he will say to those on his left, "Depart from me, you who are cursed, into the eternal fire prepared for the devil and his angels. For I was hungry and you gave me nothing to eat, I was thirsty and you gave me nothing to drink, I was a stranger and you did not invite me in, I needed clothes and you did not clothe me, I was sick and in prison and you did not look after me." They also will answer, "Lord, when did we see you hungry or thirsty or a stranger or needing clothes or sick or in prison, and did not help you?" "He will reply, "Truly I tell you, whatever you did not do for one of the least of these, you did not do for me." Then they will go away to eternal punishment, but the righteous to eternal life. (Matthew 25:31-46 NIV).

God's devotion to His firstborn is affirmed again in a judgment that takes place at a future time in the Valley of Jehoshaphat. It is spoken of in Matthew 25 and is specific to the Jewish people.

Often misquoted and used to impart a heart for the poor and the needy, this future event occurs upon Yeshua's return before entering the Kingdom of Heaven, or the Messianic age.

For more clarification, and as noted, the nations are brought into a valley outside Jerusalem that is formed by three hills and shaped like a throne seat. It is called the Valley of Jehoshaphat.

Those gathered for this judgment are the Gentile nations called sheep and goats. The goat Gentile nations are those who have mistreated the Jewish people; the sheep Gentile nations are those who supported, fed, and protected the Jewish people, Messiah's brothers, during the great and dreadful tribulation period.

For greater context, this takes place at the end of the Tribulation period to determine who enters the Messianic Kingdom during the last half of the Great Tribulation. Amid this profound period of anguish, the non-Jewish nations aligned with the antichrist's regime partake in the persecution of the Jewish people, thus relinquishing their opportunity to enter the Messianic Kingdom.

Those according to the flesh and natural seed of Abraham are Yeshua's brethren, the Jewish people (Matthew 10:6; John 1:11). Throughout the book of Acts, Paul addresses his Jewish brothers forty-five times. In almost every instance, he speaks to a Jewish audience, his brothers.

We should note that salvation is first and always in the belief in Yeshua. But the actions of this later group, *the goat*

Gentiles, is simply damning evidence of their allegiance to the antichrist. For this reason, they join in the most horrific persecution of the Jewish people ever in human history.

In closing, review the following passages of the extraordinary role that the Gentile has in the cause of Zion. Let us pray that God continues to move upon the hearts of nations to fulfill the church's end-days mandate to *"all Israel."*

Gentiles are seen as gathers of the exiles: *"'But now I will send for many fishermen,' declares the Lord, 'and they will catch them...'"* (Jeremiah 16:16 NIV).

Gentiles are guiding the Jews back to Jerusalem: *"This is what the Sovereign Lord says: 'See, I will beckon to the nations [Gentiles], I will lift up my banner to the peoples; they will bring your sons in their arms and carry your daughters on their hips'"* (Isaiah 49:22 NIV).

Gentiles are drawn to Israel:

> *And the Gentiles shall see thy righteousness, and all kings thy glory: and thou shalt be called by a new name, which the mouth of the Lord shall name. Thou shalt also be a crown of glory in the hand of the Lord, and a royal diadem in the hand of thy God. Thou shalt no more be termed Forsaken; neither shall thy land any more be termed Desolate: but thou shalt be called Hephzibah, and thy land Beulah: for the Lord delighteth in thee, and thy land shall be married* (Isaiah 62:2-4 KJV).

And the Gentiles shall come to thy light, and kings to the brightness of thy rising. Lift up thine eyes round about, and see: all they gather themselves together, they come to thee... (Isaiah 60:3-4 KJV).

The nations will be drawn to the Glory of Israel.

Gentiles recognizing God's favor on the Jews: *"This is what the Lord Almighty says: 'In those days ten men from all languages and nations will take firm hold of one Jew by the hem of his robe and say, "Let us go with you, because we have heard that God is with you"'"* (Zechariah 8:23 NIV).

Gentiles provoking the Jews to envy: *"Again I ask: Did they stumble so as to fall beyond recovery? Not at all! Rather, because of their transgression, salvation has come to the Gentiles to make Israel envious"* (Romans 11:11 NIV).

Gentiles sharing with the Jews of their material blessings: *"They were pleased to do it, and indeed they owe it to them. For if the Gentiles have shared in the Jews' spiritual blessings, they owe it to the Jews to share with them their material blessings"* (Romans 15:27 NIV).

14

THE ONE NEW MAN

IN CONSIDERING THE ONE NEW MAN, AND UNDERSTANDING it in Paul's day, the early believing Jews could never have envisioned Gentile believers outside of the citizenship of Israel. Equally, Paul could never have envisioned believing Jews outside of the citizenship of the New Covenant body, the church, particularly since it started with Jews.

Central to the One New Man is a reconstructive work of the family of God. Then as now, it demolishes walls and restores family structure. No other model in Scripture demonstrates the right relationship between the Jew and Gentile and what God intended in the days of Paul and our modern day.

Fundamentally, the scriptural teaching is that Yeshua devised in Himself a unique unity for Jew and Gentile, one unencumbered with cultural and religious regulations of man. This was also demonstrated to rulers and authorities in the heavenly realms (Ephesians 3:10). These are spoken of in Ephesians and comprise the three heavens (2 Corinthians 12:2).

One heaven is over the earth, the place of our habitation; the second is the underworld, where Satan resides and demons dwell; the third is Heaven, where God's throne resides. All of these spiritual realms were to witness the plan of the One New Man, which was to be demonstrated through the church, the material body.

TRADITIONAL TEACHING

Throughout Christian teaching, the One New Man has always focused upon a spiritual truth only. This process occurs upon salvation when Jew or Gentile becomes a new spiritual creation, or a One New Man in the traditional Christian and spiritual view.

But this traditional view alone wipes out the principle of distinction that we have maintained throughout this work and ignores the cultural and religious walls that separated Jew from Gentiles...again, the One New Man brings walls down and restores the family.

Taking the One New Man into our modern day, it differs only in the types of walls. For instance, two thousand years ago, it was Judaism's walls. Today it is Christianity's walls. Yet, the Gentiles are as enthusiastic and excited about it as they were in Paul's day.

To the Gentile, they are rediscovering a place in the "citizenship" of this "Greater Israel," a place obscured throughout Christian church history. They enjoin themselves to the Jew and freely take part in the biblical feasts, festivals, and the biblical Sabbath (Saturday Shabbat), and become sharers in a common destiny; it is a Ruth-type calling, and a *life flow* in this *Spiritual Common Wealth of Israel.*

At its core, the Gentile is recapturing the Jewish *root of New Covenant faith.* But as we shall see later, this is nothing less than a restorative reality of the Kingdom on earth and a shadow of the Kingdom to come.

CULTURAL PRESSURE IN THE DAYS OF PAUL

Traveling back in time two thousand years ago, many rabbinic regulations and a strong cultural bias kept Jews and Gentiles apart (Acts 10:28). Gentiles were referred to as dogs (Mark 7:27-28); they were forbidden in the court of the Israelites (Acts 21:28-29) or they could suffer death as a result.

Shammai, a major Jewish leader in Paul's day, enacted eighteen ordinances calling for a strict separation between Jews and Gentiles even though his rulings were considered extreme even then.

There was also the law of *covenant proselytes.* This was how Gentiles could become partakers in the commonwealth of Israel if they submitted to circumcision, underwent *mikvah* (baptism), and brought sacrifices to the temple. Only then could a Gentile become as a native-born Israelite and enjoy equal rights in all respects with native-born Jews. In Scripture, they are called proselytes (*gerim),* which are mentioned in Leviticus 17–25 and described by Philo, as ones who become naturalized into a new and godly commonwealth.

Consider also what an unlikely candidate Paul was as the torchbearer of the One New Man. He was one of the strongest and most violent enemies of the early body of believers. He also became a source of contempt for the unbelieving Jews (Acts 17), following his faith in Messiah.

More interesting, there weren't two frameworks of Christian living as today—one through the institutional Christian church, and the other through the restored Jewish root that we call Hebraic life.

In Paul's day, there was no Sunday Sabbath, Christian holy days, or Christianity, as we understand it today. Paul envisioned only one stream by which Jew and Gentile would flow in—the mystery plan of the One New Man.

Paul writes to the Ephesians to teach them that through Yeshua the dividing wall of hostility is no more. Jews and Gentiles are now united by faith in the Jewish Messiah, and all the regulations are cancelled; the door of the temple is open to all.

ABRAM BECOMES ABRAHAM

Journeying further back, we find ourselves in Genesis 17, the place where Abraham's call is recorded, and the first shadow of the One New Man. First review the dramatic events surrounding Abraham's call:

Two rows of slaughtered animals trimmed and arranged in precise order as Abraham fights off birds of prey encircling overhead waiting to swoop down. Abraham then falls into a deep sleep and something remarkable happens, God comes and walks in the midst of the sacrifice to strike an unchanging pact, but not with a single man, but rather with an entire people. God changed Abram's name to Abraham that day: *"Neither shall thy name anymore be called Abram, but thy name shall be Abraham; for a father of many nations have I made thee"* (Genesis 17:5 KJV).

The Wisdom of Abraham's Name

Always when one was given a new name in Scripture it was deeply prophetic. The most well-known was when Jacob's name was changed to Israel. With Abraham, God remodeled society in a most fundamental way—both Jew and Gentile would both look back to Abraham as their spiritual father, and an early picture of a unified family is seen (Galatians 3:8-9,14,16; Genesis 17:5).

When God changed Abram's name to Abraham, the fifth letter of the Hebrew alphabet, Hey ה, was used. This gave the "h" sound in the name *Abraham*. But the meaning of the letter is to *behold* or *reveal,* and it is always an important light into a new truth.

For instance, Psalm 133:1-3 (NKJV) begins with this letter, and a glorious truth is revealed:

> *Behold, how good and how pleasant it is for brethren to dwell together in unity! It is like the precious oil upon the head, running down on the beard, the beard of Aaron, running down on the edge of his garments. It is like the dew of Hermon, descending upon the mountains of Zion; for there the Lord commanded the blessing—life forevermore.*

THE NUMBER 248

What adds further intrigue is that each Hebrew letter possesses a numeric value. Notably, when the Hebrew letter *hey* is added to Abraham's name, it increases to 248—a composite number where the sum of its parts equals the whole. Similarly, the combination of the Jew and Gentile, with their unique attributes, forms a unified entity known as the One New Man, where the sum of their individual parts completes the whole of the family of God.

Furthermore, the entirety of a man's body consists of 248 primary components. The Torah encompasses 248 commandments, which include positive deeds and emotions. Complying with these commandments leads to complete devotion to God. Lastly, the numerical value of the *Shema* (Jewish prayer), "Hear O Israel the Lord your God, the Lord is One, blessed be your Kingdom forever," is 248. Therefore, 248 signifies unity and completeness.

A WHOLE BODY

The significance is obvious. Abram was complete when the Gentiles came into his lineage. Abraham was not just called to the Gentiles to be completed; the Gentiles had to enter into his lineage to complete him. Today, the Jew must enter the church body to complete her.

This concept of creation, or the enigma, consists of two distinct groups of individuals who unite as a single entity—Jews and Gentiles—to form the One New Man. However, this profound understanding remained concealed until

Paul experienced a divine intervention that awakened his awareness.

Dear reader, divine providence has once again been stirred to action. Numerous individuals now carry the torch of this new era. Despite the adversary's attempts to impede its progress, the foundation of the One New Man has firmly taken root within the body of end-time believers today.

FINAL WORD ON THE ONE NEW MAN

In our present day, the One New Man will serve as a significant source of grace and favor for the entire body, fulfilling various purposes.

The Hebrew letter *hey*, representing the number five, symbolizes divine favor and points to God's grace. Abram's name lacked five letters until he became a unique unity of two distinct groups—Jews and Gentiles.

To the church, the One New Man stands as a model for complete unity in the end times as taught previously. Wholeness is derived from the root word *holy,* which signifies an undivided, unified state constituting the entirety. It is crucial to consider these words: For if the rejection of the Jews leads to the reconciliation of the world, what will their acceptance be but life from the dead? (See Romans 11:15.)

As we contemplate the relevance of the One New Man today, several factors drive its significance.

THREE END-TIME MOVES OF GOD

First, we are transitioning from the church age to the Kingdom age. The nearness of the Messiah's arrival indicates a prophetic timing, and the Gentile body is being prepared to fulfill its ultimate mandate concerning "all Israel."

Second, for the first time in modern church history, Romans 11:11 is being realized in its purpose to *"provoke the Jew to envy."* Genuine love and support from Gentiles toward Jews are essential to evoke this envy. Thus, the One New Man carries an evangelistic and restorative quality that is paramount in God's plan for the end times.

Third, since the earliest collapse of the Jewish foundation within Christianity occurred, an end-time wave is revealing what the institutional Christian church rejected—the unique relationship between Jews and Gentiles found in the One New Man. For thousands of years, the church has been a dismembered body of believers.

It is difficult for established organizations, denominations, and structured church systems to embrace alternative movements. They tend to prioritize uniformity for the sake of easy administration, which played a significant role in the Jewish communities' experience within the church. Many Jewish individuals felt marginalized and excluded from the broader church community due to its emphasis on conformity within a non-Hebraic framework.

Lastly, the One New Man embodies a Kingdom quality absent from the body thus far. Through this unity, God restores a genetic blueprint that showcases the extraordinary and symbiotic relationship between Jews and Gentiles. Essentially, God's people are reclaiming what the enemy has stolen and reestablishing their ancient rights.

CONCLUSION

NO MORE FALSEHOOD

CROSSING OVER

As widely acknowledged, the community of believers in the Messiah is currently undergoing a significant and historic transformation. Certain segments of this community are shifting from a predominantly horizontal approach, influenced by a Greek Hellenistic model, to a vertical approach linked to a Kingdom and Hebraic model. This transition signifies a movement from the church era to the Kingdom era.

A mere two decades ago, discussing different parts of the community as distinct cultures with their own unique holy days and conceptual frameworks for Christian living was uncommon. However, with a fresh understanding of ancient truths, the community is now being equipped to fulfill its mandate concerning "all Israel" and the "Jewish People" in the final days.

The barriers that once separated Jews from Gentiles are being dismantled. There is also an increasing awareness of the demonic origins of replacement and dispensationalist ideologies, leading to an affirmation of the theological rights of Jews to be in Israel and to embrace their Jewish identity.

Nonetheless, the adversary is actively opposing these developments. Where God is tearing down walls, the adversary erects new barriers or reinforces existing ones. His aim is to undermine and obstruct God's progress. Nevertheless, this movement will continue to gather strength, becoming a powerful force that transforms the community of believers for the end times.

Unfortunately, the church, as the living embodiment of the Messiah, has become a central battleground for this conflict. After all, where else should this struggle take place? The church is where the mysterious plan was intended to be unveiled.

SEEING WITH FRESH PERSPECTIVE

As God grants new spiritual insight, former principles and precepts are gaining new clarity today. Aspects that were once obscured due to anti-Semitism and the removal of Jewish understanding from the New Testament are now being revealed. The Christian environment, which was previously opposed to Jewish identity, now holds deep respect for the Jewish foundation of New Covenant faith. Healing is carried on the wings of the Spirit more profoundly than ever before.

What God intended between Jew and Gentile, in a mutually beneficial relationship, and what has been dormant for centuries, is springing back to life. This revitalization will empower and position the end-time body for God's ultimate purposes—the final harvest of Zion.

For this reason, *Thy Kingdom Come* has sought to reintroduce the body to Kingdom principles and offer a preview of the coming age. As many earnestly seek the ancient paths, numerous individuals are searching for the right way and then walking in it. Therefore, our prayers and intercessions are focused on a multiplication of those who possess the courage to ask, seek, and walk in this path.

In closing, let us pray using the words taught by our Messiah, "Our Father who is in Heaven, hallowed be Your name. Your Kingdom come, Your will be done, on earth as it is in Heaven." Together, Jew and Gentile will activate the Kingdom in a new light—the light of our Father's intended purpose.

APPENDIX

THE COVENANT

COVENANTAL PROVISIONS CAME NEVER THROUGH AGREE-ments or goodwill or between man and man, but always between God and man. Predictably, it continuously involved a clash with other people. In 1948, when the Jewish people returned to their land again, it came by way of opposition and violence. Israel had to settle the whole business by force when they were attacked by an Arab League of Nations.

In ancient times in the land of Canaan, Abraham and his clan moved between two powerful heathenish cultures—Babylonia and Egypt. Later, the patriarch Abraham was brought into the War of the Kings (Genesis 14). It was a conflict comprised of an alliance of five kings that what would ultimately sweep away his nephew Lot and his household. But Abraham is seen walking as a conqueror because God gave him a promise of everlasting possession for him and all his generations. Similar circumstances befell Joshua when he had to take hold of the promise.

As the world forever struggles in formulating a definition over Israel's right to the Promised Land, the land of Israel was given to the Jewish people not as a reward and not as a freewill gift. It was also not independent of Israel's choices, for the blessings were dependent upon her obedience to Adonai. Obedience was always the key to the covenantal provisions that God promised Abraham and his generations.

King Solomon found this out when the Lord became angry with Solomon because he became lofty and willfully disobedient and carnally minded toward the forbidden women of other nations. The Lord said to Solomon, *"Since this is your attitude and you have not kept my covenant and my decrees, which I commanded you, I will most certainly tear the kingdom away from you and give it to one of your subordinates"* (1 Kings 11:11 NIV). The covenantal key and its blessings were taken from Solomon to be handed to another.

Another example is Hilkiah, the priest. Hilkiah found the lost book of the law that had been given through Moses. He began to inquire of the Lord for himself and for the remnant in Israel and Judah about what was written in this book. He said that the Lord's anger had been poured out on them because they had not kept the word of the Lord; they had not acted in accordance with all that was written in the book.

But consider, no nation other than Israel can trace their claim to a historical document as the Covenant, which the One True God Himself inscribed. No other person as Abraham and his heirs was chosen to be custodians of its provisions. Yet obedience was always the key to unlock the provisions and blessings of the Covenant that God made with Abraham and his heirs.

Since the covenants were either signed in blood or decreed by God's Word (the Noahic and Davidic covenants were decreed), they all shared an *unconditional* and *perpetual quality* that went from one generation to the next; this speaks even for our modern day. Of course, to receive the blessings of the covenants always required obedience. Therefore, the covenant was always waiting for a righteous generation to turn on its blessings.

> *Hear, Israel, and be careful to obey so that it may go well with you and that you may increase greatly in a land flowing with milk and honey, just as the Lord, the God of your ancestors, promised you* (Deuteronomy 6:3 NIV).

THE COVENANT TRANSMITTED

Covenant comes from the Hebrew word *berith,* which we have discussed in previous chapters. This word is used throughout the Hebrew Scriptures well over two hundred times. Covenants in the Bible were a formal agreement; Jacob and Laban made a covenant with each other with specific terms to be honored in their relationship (Genesis 31:44 NIV). David and Jonathan struck a *berith* in their friendship (1 Samuel 18:3, 20:8,16; 22:8; 23:18 NIV). Abner struck a *berith* with David over his loyalty to him as king (2 Samuel 3:12-13).

In Psalm 55:20 (NIV), a *berith* is referred to between friends: *"My companion attacks his friends; he violates his covenant."* Proverbs 2:17 (NIV) states, *"Who has left the partner of her youth and ignored the covenant she made before God."* These covenants formed a bond between two people, between nations, between God and a single man, and between God and a specific nation, such as Israel.

As the covenant was transmitted to Isaac then to Jacob, it provided a striking assurance of restoration to the land with God's assurance that His promises will be fulfilled: *"I am with you and will watch over you wherever you go, and I will bring you back to this land. I will not leave you until I have done what I have promised you"* (Genesis 28:15 NIV).

> *And the Lord said to Abram, after Lot had separated from him: "Lift your eyes now and look from the place where you are—northward, southward, eastward, and westward; for all the land which you see I give to you and your descendants forever. And I will make your descendants as the dust of the earth; so that if a man could number the dust of the earth, then your descendants also could be numbered. Arise, walk in the land through its length and its width, for I give it to you"* (Genesis 13:14-17 NKJV).

This is reiterated again in the Davidic covenant where God states:

> *And I will provide a place for my people Israel and will plant them so that they can have a home of their own and no longer be disturbed. Wicked people will not oppress them anymore, as they did at the beginning and have done*

ever since the time I appointed leaders over my people Israel. I will also subdue all your enemies. I declare to you that the Lord will build a house for you (1 Chronicles 17:9-10 NIV).

THE LAND COVENANT

The second part of the land aspect of the covenant is wrongly referred to as the Palestinian Covenant because it is a term coined by the Romans after the destruction of Jerusalem in the year 70, which means Philistine. Its purpose was to scorn the Jewish people with a title of their archenemies. Therefore, the word Palestine is not found in the Bible. The land covenant is located in Deuteronomy 30:1-10. The following is an overview:

- Israel will be scattered due to their disobedience (Deuteronomy 30:1).

- Israel will also repent while in their wandering (Deuteronomy 30:2).

- The Lord promises to return the remnant (Deuteronomy 30:3).

- The Lord promises to restore the remnant (Deuteronomy 30:4-5).

- The Lord promises Israel national regeneration (Deuteronomy 3:6).

- The Lord promises Israel's enemies will be judged (Deuteronomy 30:7).

- The Lord promises Israel will again prosper (Deuteronomy 30:9).

- The Lord guarantees Israel's fulfillment (Deuteronomy 30:8-10).

In Genesis 17:1-8 (KJV) God states:

And when Abram was ninety years old and nine, the Lord appeared to Abram, and said unto him, I am the Almighty God; walk before me, and be thou perfect. And I will make my covenant between me and thee, and will multiply thee exceedingly. And Abram fell on his face: and God talked with him, saying, as for me, behold, my covenant is with thee, and thou shalt be a father of many nations. Neither shall thy name any more be called Abram, but thy name shall be Abraham; for a father of many nations have I made thee. And I will make thee exceeding fruitful, and I will make nations of thee, and kings shall come out of thee. And I will establish my covenant between me and thee and thy seed after thee in their generations for an everlasting covenant, to be a God unto thee, and to thy seed after thee. And I will give unto thee and to thy seed after thee, the land wherein thou art a stranger, all the land of Canaan, for an everlasting possession; and I will be their God.

Here, God reveals specifically that the land of Israel was not given as a short-term possession, but for the Jew's personal occupation forever: "All the land that you see I will give to you and your offspring *forever*". The word *forever,* which we discussed earlier, comes from the Hebrew word *olam.*

It is the same word used in many places including Psalm 89:35-36, which states, *"His seed shall endure **forever,** and his throne as the sun before me"* (emphasis mine). This is significant because the nations have long downgraded this legal instrument to something no longer relevant and part of a past age and dispensation. Meditate on these words:

> *Yet in spite of this, when they are in the land of their enemies, I will not reject them or abhor them so as to destroy them completely, breaking my covenant with them. I am the Lord their God. But for their sake I will remember the covenant with their ancestors whom I brought out of Egypt in the sight of the nations to be their God. I am the Lord* (Leviticus 26:44-45 NIV).

Abraham's Signing Ceremony

> *So the Lord said to him, "Bring me a heifer, a goat and a ram, each three years old, along with a dove and a young pigeon." Abram brought all these to him, cut them in two and arranged the halves opposite each other; the birds, however, he did not cut in half. Then birds of prey came down on the carcasses, but Abram drove them away. As the sun was setting, Abram fell into a deep sleep, and a thick and dreadful darkness came over him. Then the Lord said to him, "Know for certain that your descendants will be*

strangers in a country not their own, and they will be enslaved and mistreated four hundred years. But I will punish the nation they serve as slaves, and afterward they will come out with great possessions. You, however, will go to your fathers in peace and be buried at a good old age. In the fourth generation your descendants will come back here, for the sin of the Amorites has not yet reached its full measure." When the sun had set and darkness had fallen, a smoking fire-pot with a blazing torch appeared and passed between the pieces. On that day the Lord made a covenant with Abram and said, "To your descendants I give this land, from the river of Egypt to the great river, the Euphrates—the land of the Kenites, Kenizzites, Kadmonites, Hittites, Perizzites, Rephaites, Amorites, Canaanites, Girgashites and Jebusites" (Genesis 15:9-21).

NOTES

AUTHOR'S NOTE

1. Susan Stroomenbergh-Halpern, *Memoirs of the War Years – The Netherlands 1940-1945, A Christian Perspective* (New York: Vantage Press, Inc., 2002).

INTRODUCTION

1. Emil Schurer, DD, MA, *A History of The Jewish People,* Volume 1, Third Edition (Peabody, MA: Hendrickson Academic, 1998).

2. Ibid.

1   JERUSALEM AND THE LAND OF ISRAEL

1. Jack Friedman, *The Jerusalem Book of Quotations: A 3,000 –Year Perspective* (Lynbrook, NY: Gefen Publishing House, 2007).

2. Richard Bell, *The Other Case For Defensible Borders* (Jerusalem: Carta,1978) and Menachem Begin, *Jerusalem, The Revolt* (Los Angeles: Nash Publishing, 1948).

3. Rabbi Hayim Halevy Donin, *To Be A Jew* (New York: Basic Books Publishers, 1972).

2 JEWISH PERSECUTION: THE STRATEGY OF SATAN

1. The Hebrew English Edition of the Babylonian Talmud; *Tractate Berakoth.*

2. Martin Gilbert, *The Atlas Of Jewish History* (New York: William Morrow and Company, 1969).

3. Abram Leon Sachar, *A History of the Jews,* Fifth Edition (New York: Alfred A. Knopf, 1967), 251.

4. *Your People Shall Be My People,* workbook by Don Finto.

5. Dennis Prager and Joseph Telushkin, *Why the Jews: The Reason for Antisemitism* (New York: A Touch Stone Book, Simon & Schuster, 1983).

6. *Der Stürmer* (literally *The Stormer* or more accurately *The Attacker*) was a weekly Nazi newspaper published by Julius Streicher from 1923 to the end of World War II in 1945. Streicher achieved a position of great wealth and influence in Nazi Germany. Der Stürmer's crude anti-Jewish invective provided a focus for Hitler's persecutory racial policies. "Julius Streicher," June 6, 2023, *Britannica.com;* https://www.britannica.com/biography/Julius-Streicher#ref52795; accessed July 30, 2023.

7. Rabbi Lee J. Levinger, *The Story of the Jew* (New York: Behrman House, Inc., 1928) and David A. Altshuler, *Hitler's War Against the Jews* (New York: Behrman House, Inc., 1978).

3 JEWISH IMMIGRATION: JEWS COME TO AMERICA

1. Arthur Hertzberg, *The Jews in America: Four Centuries of an Uneasy Encounter* (New York: Simon and Schuster, 1989), 24.

2. Rose G. Lurie, *American Jewish Heroes* (The Union of American Hebrew Congregations, 1968).

3. Ibid.

4. Prager and Telushkin, *Why the Jews.* Hertzberg, *The Jews in America.*

5. Hertzberg: *The Jews in America.*

6. Seth S. Wenger, *The Jewish Americans: Three Centuries of Jewish Voices in America* (New York: Doubleday Publishers, 2007).

7. Louis Harap, *The Image of the Jew in American Literature* (Philadelphia, PA: The Jewish Publication Society, 1974).

8. Gordon W. Allport, *The Nature of Prejudice* (Reading, MA: Addison-Wesley Publishing Co.).

4   PRINCIPLES OF ZION: BIBLICAL PRINCIPLES OF JEWISH SURVIVAL

1. "Inalienable Rights" was defined as "Rights which are not capable of being surrendered or transferred without the consent of the one possessing such rights" (according to *Morrison v. State*, Mo. App., 252 S.W.2d 97, 101). Unalienable rights are those that are "incapable of being alienated, that is, sold and transferred." It meant under no circumstances could one's rights be given to another. *Black's Law Dictionary*, 6th Edition (St. Paul, MN: West Publishing Co. 1990) 2nd Law of Zion: William R. Koenig, *Eye to Eye: Facing the Consequences of Dividing Israel* (Alexandria, VA: About Him Publishing, 2017).

2. https://www.encyclopedia.com/history/united-states-and-canada/us-history/english-common-law; accessed August 1, 2023.

3. *Black's Law Dictionary*, 6th Edition (St. Paul, MN: West Publishing Co. 1990).

4. "What are Unalienable Rights?, *ConstitutionUS.com;* https://constitutionus.com/constitution/rights/what -are-unalienable-rights/; accessed August 1, 2023.

5. Dan Senor and Saul Singer, *Start-Up Nation: The Story of Israel's Economic Miracle* (New York: Twelve Publishing, 2009).

6. Ernest Van Den Haag, *The Jewish Mystique* (New York: Stein and Day Publishers, 1969).

5   Unlocking Israel's Election

1. "Election within the Bible is the notion that God favors some individuals and groups over others, an idea that finds fullest expression in the Hebrew Bible's affirmation, supported in the New Testament, that Israel is God's chosen people": John S. Kaminsky and Joel N. Lohr, "Election in the Bible," *Oxford Bibliographies,* March 10, 2023; https://www.oxfordbibliogrphies. com/display/document/obo-9780195393361/obo -9780195393361-0250.xml; accessed August 1, 2023.

2. "The Epistle of Barnabas," translation in Holmes edition of *The Apostolic Fathers* (2007), 270-327.

6   The Battle for Israel and the Messianic Kingdom

1. Deuteronomy 32:8: *"When the Most High gave the nations their inheritance, when he divided all mankind, he set up boundaries for the peoples according to the number of the sons of Israel."* Here one can presume that when Messiah returns, He will finally settle Israel securely into their land, and also will settle the nations within their God-given boundaries (Acts 17:26). *Tractate Sanhedrin* (London: Soncino Press, 1994) (Hebrew-English Edition of the Babylonian Talmud). Sanhedrin was the council of state and supreme tribunal of the Jewish people during the century of or more preceding

the fall of the Second Temple. It consisted of seventy-one members, and was presided by over by the High Priest.

8   THE BIBLICAL FEASTS: KINGDOM TIMES AND RHYTHMS

1. Occasions when Christ spoke during the Feasts: Passover (Matthew 26:1-2, 17-29; Mark 14:12-26; Luke 22:7-38; John 2:13-25; 11:55-56; 13:1-30; 1 Corinthians 5:7). Tabernacles (John 7:2-37). Sabbath (Matthew 12:1-14; Mark 2:23-35; Luke 4:16-30; 6:1-10; 13:10-16; 14: 1-5; John 5:1-15; 9:1-34; Acts 13:14-48). Yom Kippur (Acts 27:9; Romans 3:24-26; Hebrews 9:1-14; 23-26). Feast of Dedication (John 10:22-39). Festival of Weeks—Pentecost (Acts 2:1-41; 20:16; 1 Corinthians 15:16:8). Unleavened Bread (Matthew 26:17; Mark 14:1,12; Luke 22:1,7; Acts 12:3; 20:6; 1 Corinthians 5:6).

2. Abraham Joshua Heschel, *The Allegorization of the Bible;* https://www.scribd.com/document/40071458/ Allegorization-of-Bible#; accessed August 4, 2023.

PART II   CONSTANTINE'S INTERFERENCE

1. Christianity the Empire Religion: Christianity began as a religion of the state of Rome. It was politically and economically convenient to join. It was under a single supreme authority, Emperor Constantine; it developed into a large commercial organization even then. It was the first shadow on earth of the One World Order-One World Religion.

9   THE JEWISH ROOT SEVERED

1. "The speech in Defense of Lucius Flaccus," *Cicero* (Loeb Classical Library,) volume 10, 441. David H. Stern, *Restoring the Jewishness of the Gospel. Jewish New*

Testament was an ecclesiastical synod held in Elvira in what was then the Roman province of Hispania Baetica, which ranks among the more important provincial synods, for the breadth of its canons. Its date cannot be determined with exactness but is believed to be in the first quarter of the fourth century, approximately 305-306. It was one of three councils, together with the Synod of Arles and the Synod of Ancyra that first approached the character of general councils and prepared the way for the first ecumenical council. Information taken from http://en.wikipedia.org/wiki/Synod_of_Elvira; accessed August 2, 2023.

2. David H. Stern, *Restoring the Jewishness of the Gospel: A Message for Christians* (Clarksville, MD: Lederer Books, 2010).

3. Bruce R. Booker, *The Lie: Exposing the Satanic Plot Behind Anti-Semitism* (Columbus, GA: Brentwood Academic Press, 1993).

4. *Encyclopedia Judaica* online: Publications, Inc., 1988. Synod of Elvira.

5. Richard Booker, *How the Cross Became a Sword* (Woodlands, TX: Sounds of the Trumpet, Inc., 1994).

6. Michael Brown, *Our Hands Are Stained With Blood* (Shippensburg, PA: Destiny Image Publishers, 1992).

10 THEOLOGICAL THEFTS AND FURTHER SEPARATION

1. Daniel Gruber, *The Church and the Jews: The Biblical Relationship* (Hanover, NH: Elijah Publishing, 1997).

2. Philip Schaff, *History of the Christian Church, Volume 2* (Peabody, MA: Hendrickson Publishers, 1996).

3. Ibid.

11   SABBATH AND TORAH

1. William Whiston, *The Works of Josephus* (Peabody MA: Hendrickson Publishers, 1987); *Jewish Antiquities* 11.346.

2. Philo, *The Special Laws* II, p. 574, Complete and Unabridged, New Updated Version.

3. Emil Schurer, DD,MA, *Life Under the Law: A History of the Jewish People in the Time of Jesus Christ, Volume II* (Peabody, MA: Hendrickson Publishers, 1998).

4. Edward A. Synan, *The Popes and the Jews in the Middle Ages* (New York: Macmillan Company, 1965).

5. Richard Booker, *No Longer Strangers.*

GLOSSARY

Adonai: Hebrew name of God meaning "my Lord"

Adonai Elohenu: The Lord our God

Adon olam: Eternal Lord

Amidah Prayer: The standing prayer known as *shemoneh esreh* or the "eighteen benedictions."

Antinomianism: The belief that faith frees a person from all obligations to observe the law of God. It can also be seen in an attitude of hostility toward God's law.

Benei Yisrael: Children of Israel

Chofesh: Freedom, liberty

Commonwealth: A people united by a common interest such as a state or nation (Israel). Today, Gentiles are once becoming part of this commonwealth of Israel.

Diaspora: The Greek word meaning dispersion; has been applied to all Jewish people and communities outside of Israel.

Eliyahu ha-Navi: Elijah the prophet

Elohim: God

El Shaddai: God Most High

Erets Yisrael: Land of Israel

Ha-Shem: The Name (of God)

Ivri: Means Hebrew

Ivrim: The Hebrews

Mitzvah: The Hebrew word of commandment or good deed

Moed: Appointment, fixed time or season

Moedim: Plural for Moed, and speaks of all the Feasts (Appointed Times)

Ru'ach: Wind, air, breath, soul, spirit

Ru'ac Hayimim: Breath of life

Ru'ach Adonai: Breath of God

Ruach HaKodesh: Holy Spirit

Shabbat: The Hebrew word for Sabbath

Siddur: The Jewish prayer book

Shema: Hear, O Israel

Tanakh: The Hebrew term for the entire Old Testament and is comprised of three sections: the Torah (first section in the Bible comprised of the Five Books of Moses); *Nevi'im,* the Hebrew prophets; and the *Ketuvim,* the Writings.

Teshuva: Repentance, return

Torah: The Hebrew term for the first five books of the Old Testament known as the Five Books of Moses.

Yisrael: He who strives with God, may God rule

Yeshua: Yeshua is the original Hebrew proper name for Jesus of Nazareth. In Hebrew, Yeshua means both "Salvation" and the form of Yahoshua, the "L-RD who is Salvation."

BIBLIOGRAPHY

Booker, Richard. *Blow the Trumpet in Zion*. Destiny Image Publishers, 1985.

Booker, Richard. *No Longer Strangers*. Sounds of the Trumpet, 2002.

Bridger, David, ed. and Rabbi Samuel Wolk. *The New Jewish Encyclopedia*. Behrman House Inc., 1976.

Cohn-Sherbock, Dan. *Dictionary of Jewish Biography*. Oxford University Press, 2005.

Donin, Rabbi Hayim Halevy. *To Be a Jew*. Basic Books Publishers, 2001.

Fackenheim, Emil. *To Mend the World*. Indiana University Press, 1994.

Finto, Don. *Your People Shall Be My People*. Chosen Books, 2016.

Flint, Peter W. *The Bible at Qumran: Text, Shape, and Interpretation*. Wm. B. Eerdmans Publishing Co., 2001.

Foley, Michael P. *Wedding Rites: A Complete Guide to Traditional Vows, Music, Ceremonies, Blessings and Interfaith Services*. Wm. B. Eerdmans Publishing Co., 2008.

Fruchtenbaum, Arnold. *The Footsteps of the Messiah*. Ariel Ministries Press, 2020.

Gersh, Harry. *When a Jew Celebrates*. Behrman House Inc., 1971.

Gilbert, Martin. *The Atlas of Jewish History*. William Morrow & Co. Inc., 1995.

Gruber, Dan. *The Church and the Jews.* Serenity Books, 2017.

Harap, Louis. *The Image of the Jew in American Literature.* Syracuse University Press, 2003.

Hertzberg, Arthur. *The Jews in America.* Simon & Schuster, 1998.

Hull, William L. *The Fall and Rise of Israel.* Zondervan Publishing House, 1954.

Intrater, Keith and Dan Juster. *Israel, the Church, and the Last Days.* Destiny Image Publishers, 2003.

Koenig, William. *Eye to Eye.* Christian Publications, 2017.

Krohn, Paysach J. *Bris Milah: Circumcision—The Covenant of Abraham.* Mesorah Publications Ltd., 1985.

Losh, Richard R. *All the People in the Bible: An A-Z Guide to the Saints, Scoundrels, and Other Characters in Scripture.* Wm. B. Eerdmans Publishing Co., 2008.

Lyman, Darryl. *Great Jews in Entertainment.* Jonathan David Publications Inc., 2005.

Margolies, Morris B. *Twenty/Twenty: Jewish Visionaries Through Two Thousand Years.* Jason Aronson Inc., 2000.

Mendes-Flohr, Paul R. and Jehuda Reinharz. *The Jew in the Modern World: A Documentary History.* Oxford University Press, 1980.

Newman, Louis E. *An Introduction to Jewish Ethics.* Pearson Education Inc., 2005.

Prager, Dennis, and Joseph Telushkin. *Why the Jews? The Reason for Anti-Semitism.* Simon & Schuster, 1983.

Samuels, Ruth. *Pathways Through Jewish History.* Ktav Publishing House Inc., 1967.

Scheinbaum, A. L. *Peninim on the Torah: An Anthology of Thought Provoking Ideas and Practical Insights on the Weekly Parsha.* Peninim Publications, 2005.

Senor, Dan and Saul Singer. *Start-Up Nation: The Story of*

Israel's Economic Miracle. Twelve Publishing, 2009.

Stroomenbergh Halpern, Susan. *Memoirs of the War Years 2008: The Netherlands, 1940-1945.*

A Christian Perspective. Vantage Press Inc., 2002.

Tcherikover, Victor. *Hellenistic Civilization and the Jews.* Hendrickson Publishers Inc., 1999.

Unterman, Alan. *Dictionary of Jewish Lore & Legend.* Thames and Hudson Inc., 1997.

Van Den Haag, Ernest. *The Jewish Mystique.* Stein and Day Publishers, 1969.

Wenger, Beth S. *The Jewish Americans.* Doubleday, 2007.

ABOUT FELIX HALPERN

FELIX HALPERN, BORN IN 1952 IN THE NETHERLANDS, moved to the United States with his family during his childhood and grew up in northern New Jersey. Before dedicating himself to full-time ministry, he built a successful career in the precious metals and diamond industries centered in New York City's International Diamond Center. Having spent nearly two decades immersed in the Orthodox and Hassidic Jewish communities, he possesses a deep understanding of the Jewish community.

Felix Halpern's Jewish heritage is deeply intertwined with resistance against the Nazis. His paternal grandfather served as an Orthodox rabbi and led his own synagogue in Germany. On the other hand, his maternal grandparents played a pivotal role in establishing one of the many underground resistance movements against Hitler in the Netherlands. It was during this time when his father gained knowledge and discovered his Messiah while hiding in the Dutch Underground after miraculously escaping from Germany.

For a significant portion of his life, Rabbi Halpern lived apart from Judaism. However, through a divine intervention by God, he was led back to his heritage with a purpose to minister to the "Lost Sheep of Israel." He refers to this experience as being a "Moses Jew," drawing a parallel to Moses who spent a large part of his life unaware of his true identity as an Israelite until later in life.

Having been raised in Replacement Theology, which teaches that the New Testament church replaces Israel and that Gentile Christians are the true Jews, Felix began to recognize the roots of anti-Semitism within this belief system. He earnestly prayed to God, seeking restoration of his Jewish understanding of the Scriptures, specifically desiring to see through the eyes of his Orthodox Jewish grandfather, who was well-versed in rabbinic teachings. After three months of fervent prayer, God responded miraculously, granting Felix a renewed vision and understanding of the Scriptures.

This restoration particularly illuminated passages related to Israel, the church, and the end times, dismantling the barriers erected by Replacement Theology and enabling a fuller comprehension of Scripture. In obedience to God's call and restoration, Felix immediately resigned from his position as vice president of sales and marketing in a multimillion-dollar international company.

Guided by God's direction, he liquidated his family's savings and retirement funds, embarking on a life of faith completely reliant on God's provision. Now, with over a decade of experiencing God's sufficiency and provision, Felix and his family bear witness to the remarkable faithfulness of God and the restoration of their Jewish heritage, which defines their lives today.

MINISTRY TODAY

Today, Felix Halpern ministers nationally and internationally, with a message of restoration between Jew and Gentile, the restoration of the Jewish root, and a strong emphasis on the election of Israel. He has authored *Restoring the Ancient Paths* for the Chinese body, which has become one the bestselling books in Taiwan. He then pioneered the first National Jewish Fellowship of the Assemblies of God and has served as its president for the first four years. He has also served as a General Presbyter for the Assemblies of God, on the AG Board of Ethnicity, and also on the board of Lost Lamb Evangelistic Association. Through God's grace and favor, in 2014 he established the first center for Jewish ministry in the Metro New York, New Jersey area called, Metro Jewish Resources.

Felix Halpern serves as International President of International Assemblies of God in Brazil, a Messianic organization, and continues to serve as a nationally appointed missionary to the Jewish people for the Assemblies of God in America. Felix, and Bonnie his wife, founded *Beth Chofesh* (House of Freedom), a Messianic congregation in the north Jersey area. They continue to fulfill their role to the body, in preparing the church for their end-time mandate, All Israel. They serve with a zeal and fervor in the spirit for the end times.

In 2019 Felix had a near-death experience from a medical error, died and experienced the glory of Heaven. He has since authored, *A Rabbi's Journey to Heaven, Heaven's Soul Cleanse, Dancing Past the Darkness,* and *31-Day Devotional of Living in the Glory.*

Bonnie Halpern

Bonnie Halpern was born in 1956 in Brooklyn and is a fellow laborer and pioneer. Bonnie also ministers with an anointing to empower women in these end times.

Growing up in a traditional Jewish home, Bonnie searched for God and had many supernatural encounters with her Messiah throughout her adolescent years. Her journey to faith is the basis of a powerful testimony today, as she shares her testimony to Jew and Gentile alike. A dedicated and successful mother of two young women, Bonnie also coaches women in the areas of household disciplines, finances, organizational skills, as well as parenting and nutrition.

Bonnie is a highly gifted speaker who brings to the body of Messiah a firm calling to release women into a Deborah anointing. She also ministers and teaches as a nutritional consultant, educating and training the body on the "Keys to Physical and Spiritual Health." Bonnie continually demonstrates her passion for maintaining the physical health of the body as well as teaching on practical and easy methods for helping believers maintain their "temples."

Felix and Bonnie Halpern have been happily married for more than three decades. They have two daughters and one grandchild. Tara is in medical school, and Heather is married and regularly works as a freelance writer for various publications. The Halperns reside in the North Jersey area of the United States.

FILMS AND BOOKS ABOUT FELIX HALPERN'S FAMILY

The University of Southern California's Shoah Foundation Institute for Visual History and Education, established by Steven Spielberg, taped a story for the United States Holocaust Memorial Museum library that included the testimony of the author's father and grandfather, an Orthodox Jewish rabbi of a synagogue in Germany. Spielberg's film shares his father's story—one of survival as an Orthodox Jewish boy escaping Nazi-occupied Germany who found himself in the hands of the Dutch underground to save him. The film is a poignant picture that testifies to the millions of Jews whose lives were forever altered, generations that were blighted from history.

Author Rabbi Halpern's maternal side claims a heritage of resistance against the Nazis. The story is chronicled in a book authored by his mother, Susan Stroomenbergh-Halpern, titled *Memoirs of the War Years: The Netherlands, 1940–1945: A Christian Perspective.* It is the story of a Dutch family's valiant efforts to launch a resistance movement against the Nazis on behalf of the Jewish people. Those efforts were recognized on December 22, 1997, at the Righteous Among the Nations Ceremony held at the Israeli Embassy in New York by Consul General Colette Avital. Rabbi Halpern's mother and maternal grandparents received medals and documents to memorialize their sacrifices.

Contact Information

Felix and Bonnie Halpern

Email: metrojrag@gmail.com

Email: hisglobalglory@gmail.com

For donations or more information, write:

Metro Jewish Resources

PO Box 3777

Wayne, NJ 07474

From

FELIX HALPERN

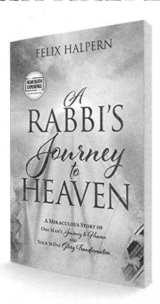

A Rabbi's Journey to Heaven

It all happened suddenly. In a twinkling of an eye. Rabbi Felix died, left his body, and crossed over into heaven. Amazed, he experienced the glories of heaven that he always read, pondered, and dreamt about. He also saw the lower realm, the second heaven, where demons dwell.

Three days after returning from heaven, God also gave Rabbi Felix a gift called "The Heavenly Soul Cleanse" which holds the keys to a transformational prayer life that turns our current prayer culture upside down. Rabbi Felix now lives from an open heaven, and as he shares these heavenly keys with you in this book, so will you. Imagine saturating your soul in heavenly glory and starving your soul from the natural order. As you do, God will heal your soul, and you will be launched into an entirely new operating system.

Take this journey with Rabbi Felix and experience this heavenly transformation. True freedom awaits you, and you will never be the same!

Purchase your copy wherever books are sold

From

FELIX HALPERN

30 Days of His Glory

It all happened suddenly. In a twinkling of an eye. Rabbi Felix died, left his body, and crossed over into heaven. Amazed, he experienced the glories of heaven that he had only read, pondered, and dreamt about.

In these extraordinary heavenly experiences, Rabbi Felix's eyes were opened to life-changing truths about the spiritual world that he shares with you.

Imagine submerging your soul in the Glory of God, and starving your soul of the natural for 30 days! For 30 days you will drown your soul in the Glory and magnification of God! You will experience heaven's operating system as it was given to Rabbi Felix. You will be launched into a daily living where you have a sky over your life and no longer a ceiling.

Heaven's Soul Cleanse is 100% biblical, and 100% centered upon the magnification and enlargement of God's glory and presence. It is guaranteed to imprint your soul and transform your mind. No longer will you be burdened by mortal pressures; no longer will you ask God repeatedly for the same thing. This new operating system will teach you to transfer ownership of your daily burdens to God, and it is 100% sustainable.

Purchase your copy wherever books are sold

In the Right Hands, This Book Will Change Lives!

Most of the people who need this message will not be looking for this book. To change their lives, you need to **put a copy of this book in their hands.**

Our ministry is constantly seeking methods to find the people who need this anointed message to change their lives. **Will you help us reach these people?**

Extend this ministry by sowing three, five, ten, or *even more* books today and change people's lives for the better! Your generosity will be part of catalyzing the Great Awakening that many have been prophesying and praying for.